ENJOYING THE PROVERBS

By
William MacDonald

Walterick Publishers
P.O. Box 2216
Kansas City, Kansas 66110

Copyright © 1965 by William MacDonald

Revised Edition
Copyright © 1982 by William MacDonald

Printed in U.S.A.

Table of Contents

Lesson	Page
1. Introduction Proverbs 1, 2	5
2. Proverbs 3—5	23
3. Proverbs 6, 7	37
4. Proverbs 8, 9	47
5. Proverbs 10—12	55
6. Proverbs 13—15	71
7. Proverbs 16, 17	89
8. Proverbs 18—20	101
9. Proverbs 21—23	115
10. Proverbs 24—26	129
11. Proverbs 27—29	143
12. Proverbs 30, 31	157

For additional information or counseling write:
Listen, My Son
P.O. Box 2216
Kansas City, Kansas 66110

Lesson One
Proverbs 1, 2

Introduction

The book of Proverbs is as modern as today. It deals with the problems of life that each of us has to face.

If any book in the Bible could be said to be beamed especially to young people, this one could. It is the world's finest collection of sound, sanctified common sense, written so that young people might not have to make some of the dreary mistakes that their elders have made.

Arnot calls the book, "Laws from heaven for life on earth." That describes its contents very concisely.

A proverb is a pithy statement of wisdom, worded in a way that makes it easy to remember. Most of the proverbs consist of two clauses, presenting either similarities or contrasts.

The fact that there are 31 chapters makes the book ideal for monthly reading—one chapter a day for every day of the month.

The book is difficult to outline. Instead of presenting a continuity of thought, like a moving picture, it presents individual pictures, like colored slides.

As you study it, you will find that it resembles the book of James in many ways. Make a list of these similarities.

Another valuable study device is to find illustrations of individual proverbs from:
1. the Bible itself
2. history
3. the daily newspaper
4. your own experience.

It will be helpful for the student to remember that while some of the proverbs are statements of absolute truth, some are statements that are generally true but that might have an exception here and there. For instance, it is always true that "the name of the Lord is a strong tower" (18:10), but there may be exceptions to the statement that "a friend loveth at all times" (17:17).

Written by Solomon and others, the book of Proverbs provides a liberal education; it covers a wide range of subjects—from spanking a child to ruling a kingdom. One sometimes wonders if there is any truth that is not found here, at least in germ form. It speaks of the liquor problem, installment buying, juvenile delinquency, and labor management. You will meet all kinds of people here—the brawling woman, the proud fool, the man who does not like to be told his faults, and the ideal wife. And best of all, the Lord Jesus is here, speaking to us as Wisdom personified. "The ideal elements in the book speak of Him; the actual shortcomings cry out for Him" (quoted in Daily Notes).

One final word of explanation! This is a self-study course designed to help you learn for yourself the wisdom of the book of Proverbs. In studying these notes, it is essential to first read the corresponding verse or verses. Many of the explanations will be meaningless unless you have read the proverb in question. The answer key for each test will be found at the back of the book. Be sure to restudy carefully each question you have missed.

Classification of Some of the Subjects in the Book of Proverbs

The Lord
  Source of wisdom, 2:6-8
  Guidance of, 3:5,6; 16:3,9
  Discipline of, 3:11,12
  Creation by, 3:19,20; 16:4; 20:12; 22:2b; 29:13b
  Confidence in, 3:25,26
  The blessing of, 10:22
  Omnipresence of, 15:3
  Omniscience of, 15:11; 16:2
  Prayer answered by, 15:8,29
  Judgment and justice by, 15:25a; 17:3; 21:2; 29:26
  Protection by, 15:25b; 18:10

Sovereignty and power of, 16:1,7,9,33; 19:21; 20:24; 21:30,31; 22:12
To be trusted, 29:25b

The fear of the Lord, 1:7, 29; 2:5; 8:13; 9:10; 10:27; 14:26, 27; 15:16, 33; 16:6; 19:23; 22:4; 23:17; 24:21; 28:14

The Word and obedience to it, 13:13, 14; 16:20; 19:16; 28:4, 7, 9; 29:18; 30:5, 6

The righteous man and wicked man contrasted, 3:32,33; 10:3, 6, 7, 9, 11, 16, 24, 25, 28, 29-32; 11:3-11, 17-21, 23, 27, 31; 12:2, 3, 5-8, 12-14, 20, 21, 26, 28; 13:2, 5, 6, 9, 21, 25; 14:2, 9, 11, 14, 22, 32; 15:8, 9, 26; 24:15, 16; 28:1, 12

The wise man and foolish man contrasted, 3:35; 10:8, 13, 14, 23; 12:15, 16, 23; 13:16; 14:1, 3, 8, 15, 16, 18, 19, 24, 33; 15:7, 14, 20, 21; 17:11, 12, 16, 21, 24, 25, 28; 18:2, 6-8; 29:8, 9, 11

Wisdom personified, 1:20-33; 8:1-36; 9:1-6; 14:1a; 16:16, 22; 19:23

The wicked woman or harlot, 2:16-19; 5:3-23; 6:24-35; 7:5-27; 9:13-18; 22:14; 23:27, 28; 30:20

Other women
  The wife of one's youth, 5:18,19
  A gracious woman, 11:16
  A beautiful woman without discretion, 11:22
  A good wife, 12:4; 18:22; 31:10-31
  A contentious woman, 19:13; 21:9,19; 25:24; 27:15,16
  A prudent wife, 19:14
  An unloved woman, 30:23

The rich man and the poor man, 10:15; 13:7,8; 14:20,21,31;

15:16; 17:1,5; 18:23; 19:1,4,17; 21:13; 22:2,7,16,22,23; 28:3,6,11,27; 29:7,13

Wealth
  Gained honestly, 10:16
  Gained dishonestly, 10:2; 13:22b; 15:6b; 20:17; 21:6; 22:16; 28:8
  Gained hastily, 13:11; 20:21; 28:20b,22
  Its limited value, 11:4
  Not to be trusted, 11:28
  Accompanied by trouble, 15:6,16,17; 16:8; 17:1
  Less valuable than wisdom, 16:16
  Protection of, 10:15a; 13:8; 18:11
  Gained by violence, 11:16
  Pretended, 13:7
  Brings friends, 19:4,6
  Inherited, 19:14
  Transient, 23:4,5; 27:24

Stewardship and generosity, 3:9,10,27,28; 11:24-26; 19:6; 21:26b; 22:9; 28:27

Gifts and bribes, 15:27; 17:8,23; 18:16; 19:6; 21:14; 25:14; 29:4

Words of parental advice, 1:8-19; 2:1-22; 3:1-35; 4:1-27; 5:1-23; 6:1-35; 7:1-27; 23:19-35; 24:4-22; 31:1-9

Obedience and disobedience to parents, 1:8,9; 6:20,22; 13:1; 19:26; 20:20; 23:22; 30:17

Instructions in child training, 13:24; 19:18; 22:6, 22:15; 23:13,14; 29:15,17

Speech
  Good, 10:20a,21a; 16:21,23,24; 23:16
  Excessive, 10:19a; 13:3b
  Restrained, 10:19b; 11:12b,13b; 12:23a; 13:3a;

17:27a,28; 21:23
Belittling, 11:12a
Talebearing, gossiping, 11:13a; 16:28; 17:9b; 18:8; 20:19; 22:11a; 26:10,22-26,28
Harmful, 11:9,11; 12:18a; 15:4b; 16:27; 18:21; 26:18,19
Healing, 12:18b; 15:4a; 16:24; 18:21
Foolish, 12:23b; 14:3a,7; 15:2b; 18:6,7
Gentle, 15:1a,4a
Harsh, 15:1b
Wise, 10:31a; 14:3b; 15:2a; 18:4
Perverse, 4:24; 10:31b,32b; 15:4b; 17:20b
Appropriate, 15:23; 25:11
Inappropriate, 17:7
Thoughtful, 15:28a
Evil, 12:13a; 15:28b
Hasty, 18:13; 29:20
Satisfying, 12:14; 18:20
Backbiting, 25:23
Lying, deceitful, 6:17; 10:18a; 12:19b,22a; 14:25b; 17:4; 26:18,19,23-26,28a
Flattering, 20:19; 26:28b; 28:23; 29:5
Disturbing, 27:14
Slanderous, 10:18b; 30:10
Honest, 12:19a; 13:5
Worthless, 14:23b

True and false witness, 6:19; 12:17; 14:5,25; 19:5,9,28; 21:28; 25:18

The diligent man and the sluggard contrasted, 10:4,5; 12:24,27; 13:4
The diligent man, 21:5; 22:29 (AV); 27:18,23-27; 28:19a
The sluggard, 6:6-11; 10:26; 15:19; 18:9; 19:15,24; 20:4,13; 21:25; 22:13; 24:30-34; 26:13-16
Industriousness, 12:9,11; 14:4,23a

Teachableness (willingness to accept instruction and correction), 1:5; 9:7-9; 10:17; 12:1,15; 13:1,10,18;

15:5,10,12,31,32; 17:10; 19:20,25; 21:11; 25:12; 27:5,6; 28:23; 29:1

The scorner or scoffer, 3:34a; 9:7,8,12; 13:1; 14:6; 15:12; 19:25; 21:11,24; 22:10; 24:9; 29:8a

The wisdom of getting guidance or advice from others, 11:14; 12:15; 15:22; 20:18; 24:6

Suretyship, 6:1-5; 11:15; 17:18; 20:16; 22:26,27; 27:13

False balances and weights, 11:1; 16:11; 20:10,23

Justice and injustice, 13:23; 17:15,26; 18:5; 21:15; 22:8,16; 24:23,24

The interrelationship between physical, mental, and spiritual health, 3:1,2,7,8,16; 4:10,22; 9:11; 13:12; 14:30; 15:13,30; 16:24; 17:22; 18:14; 27:9

Pride and humility, 3:34b; 8:13; 11:2; 15:33; 16:5,18,19; 18:12; 22:4; 29:23

Temper and patience, 14:17,29; 15:18; 16:32; 19:11

Friends, neighbors, and friendship, 3:27-29; 6:1-5; 11:12; 12:26; 14:21; 16:28; 17:9, 17; 18:17, 24; 21:10; 22:24, 25; 24:17, 19; 25:8, 9, 17, 20, 21, 22; 26:18, 19; 27:6, 9, 10, 14, 17; 28:23; 29:5

Abominations
  To the Lord, 3:32; 6:16; 8:7; 11:1,20; 12:22; 15:8,9,26; 16:5; 17:15; 20:10,23; 21:27; 28:9
  To others, 13:19; 16:12; 24:9; 26:25; 29:27

Wine, 20:1; 21:17; 23:20,21,29-35; 31:4-7

Temperance and self-control, 23:1-3; 25:28

Honey, 16:24; 24:13; 25:16,27; 27:7

The king or ruler, 14:28,35; 16:10,12-15; 19:12; 20:2,8,26,28; 21:1; 22:11,29; 23:1; 24:21,22; 25:2-7,15; 28:15,16; 29:2,4,12,14,26; 30:31; 31:4,5

Servants and slaves, 14:35; 17:2; 19:10; 29:19,21

Ancient landmarks, 22:28; 23:10,11

Enemy, 16:7; 24:17,18; 25:21; 27:6

Envy, 3:31; 14:30; 23:17; 24:1,19; 27:4

Old age, 16:31; 17:6; 20:29

The lot, 16:33; 18:18

Reputation, 10:7; 22:1

Partiality, 18:5; 24:23b-25; 28:21

Borrowing and lending, 22:7b

Soul-winning, 11:30 (AV); 24:11,12

Strife and contention, 10:12; 12:18; 13:10; 15:1-4,18; 16:27,28; 18:6-8; 21:9,19; 28:25

Bible Versions

AV   Authorized Version

ASV   The American Standard Version of the Holy Bible (1901)

RSV	The Revised Standard Version of the Holy Bible (1952)
NASB	The New American Standard Bible (1960)
NIV	New International Version
JND	The Holy Scriptures, A New Translation by J. N. Darby
LB	The Living Bible, Paraphrased
TEV	Wisdom for Modern Man, Proverbs and Ecclesiastes (Today's English Version)

Moffatt's Translation of the Bible

The New Berkeley Version of the Holy Bible

Knox's Translation of the Holy Bible

CHAPTER 1

1. Solomon was the wisest, richest, and most honored of the kings of Israel (1 Kings 3:12,13; 4:30,31). He spoke 3000 proverbs, but only some of them are preserved in this book. These extend from 1:1 to 29:27.

2. Verses 2-6 tell us why he wrote these proverbs. In brief, they provide practical wisdom for the living and management of life.

Here men may learn shrewdness and receive the kind of instruction that provides know-how. Here they may learn to discern between what is good and evil, profitable and worthless, helpful and harmful.

3. Here men are schooled in what is wise, righteous, proper, and honorable.

4. By listening to these proverbs the simple develop "savvy" and young people gain insight and sanctified commonsense.

5. Wise men will grow wiser by heeding these proverbs, and a man of discernment will learn how to guide himself and to counsel others as well. Is it not significant that a book addressed primarily to youth should announce at the very outset, "A wise man will hear"? That is what is meant by a wise man in the book of Proverbs. It is a person who is teachable. He is willing to listen and not do all the talking. He is not an insufferable know-it-all.

6. The book is designed to enable a person to understand a proverb and the lesson which often lies beneath the surface. It helps him to grasp the meaning of wise sayings and the hidden truths contained in them.

7. Now we come to the key verse of the book (see also 9:10). The fear of the Lord is the chief part of knowledge. If a man wants to be wise, the place to begin is in reverencing God and in trusting and obeying Him. What is more reasonable than that the creature should trust his Creator? On the other hand, what is more illogical than for a man to reject God's Word and to live by his own hunches? The wise thing to do is to repent of one's sins, trust Jesus Christ as Lord and Savior, and then live for Him wholeheartedly and devotedly.

Fools despise wisdom and instruction. Just as a wise man in this book is one who is willing and anxious to learn, a fool is one who cannot be told anything. He is intractable and conceited, and only learns lessons the hard way, if at all.

8. The first seven chapters are largely addressed to "my son"; the expression occurs about 15 times. In these chapters, we hear the heartbeat of a parent who wants the best in life for his child. By heeding this parental advice, a young person will avoid life's booby traps and develop expertise in practical, everyday affairs.

How much we owe to the influence of godly parents, and especially godly mothers! "Many great men of the past have been richly blessed by what they learned at their mother's knee. Consider Moses, Samuel, and Timothy. The maternal care and godly influence experienced by these spiritual leaders bore rich fruit in their lives. Think too of Augustine, John Newton, and the zealous Wesley brothers. Their names would probably never have lighted the pages of history if it hadn't been for the godly women who raised them in homes where the law of love and Christian witness was their daily guide and inspiration" (Henry G. Bosch).

9. When parental advice is followed, it becomes a graceful wreath on the head and ornaments around the neck, which is a poetic way of saying that obedience brings honor and moral beauty to the life of a wise son.

10. Often when a young man ruins his life, the explanation is given that he "got in with the wrong crowd." The process is described in verses 10-19 in living color.

First, however, the warning flag is flown. Life is full of enticements to evil. We must have the courage and backbone to say "No" a thousand times a week.

11. Here the street-corner gang invites our young friend to participate in an armed robbery. If necessary they will "bump off" the victim. Our friend may be flattered that these toughs would accept him as one of the gang. And he may be lured by the excitement of anything so daring.

12. Perhaps he is bored by a sheltered life, and wants to do something "for kicks." Well, here it is! The perfect crime! Sudden and violent death, then a quick disposal of any tell-tale evidence.

13. And the great incentive, of course, is that they will all be rich overnight. There will be enough loot to fill the houses of all the accomplices.

14. So the word is, "Get with it, and you'll make a bundle. Everyone shares equally. You can't lose."

15. But a wiser voice says, "Don't do it. Stay as far away from them as possible. Have nothing to do with their plans for instant wealth. You can't win."

16. "What you must realize is that these guys constantly pursue lives of crime, and are quick on the trigger. They commit one murder after another in rapid succession."

17. A bird has enough sense to avoid any net or snare that can be clearly seen.

18. But these men make a trap for themselves, then walk straight into it. They "lie in wait for their own blood, they set an ambush for their own lives" (RSV).

19. There is a moral to the story. Those who try to get rich quick pay for their greed with their own lives. "Such is ever the end of greed; he who cherishes it must fall by it at last" (Knox).

This particular passage deals with the attempt to get rich through violence. But the application is wider. Any get-rich-quick scheme is included, whether it be gambling, sweepstakes, or stockmarket speculation.

20. Now we enter a section of the book of Proverbs where we hear two voices calling out to men as they pass by. One is the voice of Wisdom, the other the voice of the strange woman. Wisdom, though presented here as a woman, actually symbolizes the Lord Jesus Christ. The strange woman is a type of sinful temptation and of the ungodly world.

In verses 20-33 wisdom pleads with those who foolishly think they can get along without her.

Notice that she stands in strategic places so that all men may hear her message. Now she is in the street, now in the city square.

21. Now she is at the noisy intersections, and now at the entrances of the city gates. And so it is that our Lord calls to the race of men wherever they pass by.

22. Wisdom cries to the simple, the scorners, and the foolish. The simple are naive, impressionable people who are open to all kinds of influences, both good and bad; here their instability seems to be leading them in the wrong direction. The scorners are those who treat wise counsel with contempt; nothing is sacred or serious to them. Fools are those who senselessly refuse instruction; they are conceited and opinionated in their ignorance.

23. This verse may be understood in two ways. First, it may mean, "Since you won't listen to my invitation, now turn and listen to my rebuke. I will pour out my spirit in words of judgment, and will tell you what lies ahead for you." According to this interpretation, verses 24-27 are the words which describe their fate.

The second possible meaning is this: "Turn and repent when I reprove you. If you do, then I will pour out my spirit on you in blessing, and make my words of wisdom known to you." The word "spirit" here probably means "thoughts" or "mind." While it is true that Christ pours out the Holy Spirit on those who answer His call, this truth was not as clearly stated in the Old Testament as it is in the New.

24. One of the greatest tragedies of life is the crass rejection of wisdom's gracious entreaties. It called forth the lament of lost opportunity from the summit of Olivet, "I would . . . but ye would not."

25. Wisdom sorrows over men who brush aside her advice and who will have nothing to do with her constructive criticism.

What makes man's stubborn refusal so irrational is that God's commandments and warnings are for man's good, not for God's. This is illustrated in a story which D. G. Barnhouse told. A small child squeezed past the metal railing that kept spectators six feet from the lions' cage at the Washington Zoo. When her grandfather ordered her to come out, she backed away teasingly. A waiting lion grabbed her, dragged her into the cage, and mangled her to death. The lesson is this: "God has given us commandments and principles that are for our good; God never gives us a commandment because He is arbitrary or because He doesn't want us to have fun. God says, 'Thou shalt have no other gods before me,' not because He is jealous of His own position and prerogatives, but because He knows that if we put anything, *anything* before Him, it will hurt us. If we understand the principle behind this fact, we can also understand why God chastens us. 'Whom the Lord loves, he chastens' (Heb. 12:6). He doesn't want us to back into a lion, for there is a lion, the devil, seeking whom he may devour" (Barnhouse).

26. If man persists in his refusal to listen, that rejection will inevitably bring calamity and ruin. Then it will be wisdom's turn to laugh. "I will even laugh at your calamity; I will mock when your dread comes" (NASB).

Does this mean that the Lord will actually laugh when disaster falls on the ungodly, as suggested here and in Psalm 2:4? If we think of the laughter as containing any trace of cruelty, malice, or vindictiveness, then the answer is clearly "No." Rather we should think of this laughter in a figurative way. In idiomatic language, it expresses how ludicrous and ridiculous it is for a mere man to defy the Omnipotent Sovereign, as if a gnat should defy a blast furnace. And there may also be this thought. A man may laugh at Wisdom's commandments or treat them as if they didn't exist; but when that man is reaping the harvest of his folly, the commandments still stand unmoved, and to the scorner, at least, they seem to be having the last laugh—the laugh of poetic justice.

27. Payday will surely come. The judgment men feared will descend on them like a storm. Calamity will roar down like a tornado. Distress, anguish, shock, and despair will seize them.

28. Then men will seek Wisdom in vain. They will be

desperate to find her, but won't be able to. They will realize too late that light rejected is light denied. They would not see; now they cannot see. God's Spirit will not always strive with man (Gen. 6:3). This is what gives urgency to the Gospel appeal:

Be in time! Be in time!
While the voice of Jesus calls you,
Be in time!
If in sin you longer wait,
You may find no open gate,
And your cry be just too late.
Be in time!

29. The condemnation of these scorners is that they despised Wisdom's instructions, and stubbornly refused to reverence Jehovah. Perhaps they sneered that the gospel was for women and children, but not for them. "Professing themselves to be wise, they became fools" (Rom. 1:22).

30. They had no place in their lives for the good advice contained in the Word of God, and laughed when the Scriptures condemned their ungodly words and works. They weren't afraid of God or of His judgments.

31. Now they must pay the staggering price of their wilfulness, and be glutted with the bad fruit of their own schemes. It is their own fault, not Wisdom's. They simply would not listen.

32. "For heedless folk fall by their own self-will, the senseless are destroyed by their indifference" (Moffatt). Every man is free to make his own choices in life, but he is not free to choose the consequences of his choices. God has established certain moral principles in the world. These principles dictate the consequences for every choice. There is no way to put asunder what God has thus joined together.

33. On the plus side, the one who heeds Wisdom will live in safety and in freedom from fear. Those who are Wisdom's disciples enjoy the good life, escaping the sufferings, sorrows, and shame that dog the footsteps of the wilful and the wicked.

CHAPTER 2

1. In this chapter, Solomon urges his son to walk in the ways of wisdom. The first four verses give the conditions for receiving the knowledge of God; a person must be earnest and sincere in seeking it with all his heart. The rest of the chapter promises that wisdom and discernment will be given. The 22 verses correspond to the 22 letters of the Hebrew alphabet.

First, the son is urged to take to heart his father's teaching and treasure up his commands. The proverbs were intended to be "stored up" (NIV) or memorized.

2. There must be an open ear and an open heart or mind. The son must be an attentive listener, not a compulsive talker. He is not told to talk out his problems, à la much of modern counseling; rather he should listen to the wise advice of others.

3. If he really means business, let him cry out after knowledge, and send out an appeal for understanding. Seriousness of purpose is of primary importance. It is a law of life that we get what we go after.

4. What we need is the same kind of drive that men have in mining for silver or in searching for hidden treasure. The tragedy is that too often men show more zeal in acquiring material wealth than spiritual riches.

5. But those who seek inevitably find. Those who are anxious to come into a right relationship with the Lord and to really know God are never disappointed. That is why one of the early church fathers said that the man who seeks God has already found Him.

Christ reveals the Father to all who believe on Him. To know Christ is to know God.

6. After we have been saved through faith in Christ, we are then in a position to learn divine wisdom from God. He teaches us how to think straight, how to evaluate, how to discern truth and error and how to develop divine insight.

7. He provides rich stores of wisdom for the upright, and a special shield of protection for those who walk in integrity.

8. He guards the path of those who live clean, moral lives; they escape the pain and bitterness that sin leaves in its trail. "Safe and sound the chosen friends of God come and go" (Knox).

9. This verse parallels verse 5. Both begin with "Then" and list the benefits of seriously seeking the knowledge of God.

The man who keenly desires to know and do God's will learns how to behave righteously, to act fairly, to conduct himself honestly—in short, to choose the right way every time.

10. The reason this happens is that wisdom takes control of his mind, and the knowledge of what is right becomes delightful rather than distasteful. To the true believer, God's commands are not irksome. Christ's yoke is easy and His burden is light.

11. Discretion, or the ability to make wise decisions, saves a man from many a "bad trip." Sound judgment delivers him from involvement with wicked men. None of us realizes the extent to which we are daily preserved from spiritual, moral, and physical perils. The Christian enjoys a well-guarded life, having escaped the corruption that is in the world through lust.

12. We are saved from the partnership of evil men (vv. 12-15) and from the embrace of the loose woman (vv. 16-19).

First we are saved from the world of ungodly men who misrepresent facts and distort the truth. Their speech is utterly untrustworthy.

13. These are men who leave the well-lighted streets of righteousness to slink in the dark alleys of crime and crookedness.

14. They take a savage delight in wickedness and rejoice in the way their sin turns everything topsy-turvy.

15. They follow crooked routes and their behavior is sly and devious.

16. Wisdom saves not only from the company of men like these but also from the clutches of the strange woman. We may understand this woman as a literal prostitute or we may see her as a figure of false religion or of the ungodly world.

Her method is flattery: "You aren't appreciated at home as you should be. You are so handsome, so talented. You have so much to offer. You need love and sympathetic understanding, and I'm the one to give it to you."

17. She is unfaithful to the companion of her youth, that is, her husband. She forgets the covenant of her God, that is, the marriage vows that she made before God. Or "the covenant of her God" may refer to the Ten Commandments and specifically to the seventh commandment, which forbids adultery.

18. The first clause of this verse may be translated "For her house sinks down to death" (NASB) or "she sinketh down unto death, which is her house" (RV margin). The second clause of the verse seems to support the NASB translation. Putting them together, the thought is: her house inclines to death, and therefore those who enter it are sliding toward the grave. Her paths lead to the dead, and therefore those who follow her will soon be in the realm of departed spirits.

19. Once a man is ensnared by her, it is almost impossible to escape. The verse actually seems to rule out any hope of a come-back at all. But many statements in the Bible must be understood as general rules, to which there may be a few exceptions. That is the point here. Once a man is initiated into her secrets, it is extremely hard to get back on the right road again.

20. Link this verse with the eleventh. Wisdom preserves not only from evil men and the strange woman, but, on the positive side, it encourages companionship with those who are worthwhile and upright.

21. Under the law of Moses, men of integrity were rewarded with a secure place in the land of Canaan. When we come over to the New Testament, these material blessings in earthly places give way to spiritual blessings in the heavenlies. But the fact remains that righteousness and decency are rewarded in this life as well as in the life to come.

22. It is equally true that the wicked will be cut off from the land of blessing. There is no lasting inheritance there for the treacherous.

Lesson Two
Proverbs 3—5

CHAPTER 3

1. Like all good parents, Wisdom wants the best for her children. She knows that that can come only through obedience to her teachings, which is another way of saying obedience to the sacred Scriptures. So here she pleads with her son to remember with the mind and obey with the heart.

2. In general, those who are subject to their parents live longer and better lives. Those who kick up their heels against parental discipline invite illness, accidents, tragedies and premature death. This verse thus corresponds to the fifth commandment (Exod. 20:12) which promises long life to those who honor their parents.

"The Bible teaches that a peace of mind which leads to longer, happier living comes from keeping God's commandments. A guilty conscience is a body-breaking load. A good conscience is one significant factor which leads to longevity and physical health. And so, in a measure, one's somatic (bodily) welfare stems from the welfare of his soul. A close psychosomatic connection between one's behavior before God and his physical condition is an established physical principle" (Jay Adams).

3. Lovingkindness and faithfulness should be seen in the outward behavior (bind them about thy neck) and should be true of the inward life as well (write them upon the table of thine heart).

4. This is the way to find favor and good repute (or success, AV margin) in the sight of God and man. What it boils down to is that the satisfying life is the one that is lived in the center of God's will. But that brings up the question, "How can I know God's will in my life?" A classic answer is given in the next two verses.

5. First, there must be a full commitment of ourselves—spirit, soul, and body—to the Lord. We must trust Him not only for the salvation of our souls but also for the direction of our lives. It must be a trust without reserve.

Next, there must be a healthy distrust of self, an acknowledgement that we do not know what is best for us, that we are not capable of guiding ourselves. Jeremiah expressed it pointedly: "O Lord, I know that the way of man is not in himself: it is not in man that walketh to direct his steps" (Jer. 10:23).

6. Finally, there must be an acknowledgment of the Lordship of Christ: "In all thy ways acknowledge Him." Every area of our lives must be turned over to His control. We must have no will of our own, only a single pure desire to know His will and to do it.

If these conditions are met, the promise is that God will provide the necessary guidance. He may do it through the Bible, through the advice of godly Christians, through the marvelous converging of circumstances, through the inward peace of the Spirit, or through a combination of these. But if we wait, He will make the guidance so clear that to refuse would be positive disobedience.[1]

7,8. Conceit puts us on "hold" as far as divine guidance is concerned. When we fear the Lord and turn away from evil, it means "all systems go." It spells healing to the body and refreshment to the bones. Here again we are brought face to face with the close connection between man's moral and spiritual condition and his physical health. It has been estimated that fear, sorrow, envy, resentment, hatred, guilt, and other emotional stresses account for over 60% of our illness. Add to that the terrible toll taken by alcohol (cirrhosis of the liver); tobacco (emphysema, cancer, heart disease); immorality (venereal diseases). Then we realize that Solomon,

---

[1] The clause "he shall direct thy paths" is more accurately "he shall make thy paths smooth" or "straight," but guidance is surely included in the promise.

by divine inspiration, was way ahead of his times in the field of medical science.

9,10. One way in which we can acknowledge the Lordship of Christ is in our stewardship of material things. All we have belongs to Him. We are stewards, responsible for its management. It is our privilege to choose a modest standard of living for ourselves, put everything above that to work for God, and trust God for the future. Like David Livingston, we should determine not to look upon anything we possess except in relation to the Kingdom of God.

The generous Jew in the Old Testament was promised bulging barns and overflowing vats of wine. Even though our blessings may be of a more spiritual nature, it is still true that we cannot outgive the Lord.

11,12. We can also acknowledge the Lord by submitting to His discipline. Too often we tend to think of discipline as meaning punishment, but it actually includes all that is involved in the proper training of a child, i.e., instruction, warning, encouragement, advice, correction, and spanking. Everything that God allows to come into our lives is purposeful. We should not reject it or resent it. Neither should we shrink from it or give up under it. Rather we should be concerned that God's purpose is achieved through the discipline, and thus we reap the maximum profit from it. God's ultimate purpose in the disciplines of life is that we become partakers of His holiness.

Discipline is a proof of love, not anger. Correction is a proof of sonship (see Heb. 12:6-8).

Thought—a gardener prunes grapevines but not thistles.

13. The fortunate man is the one who gets Wisdom, and especially so when we remember that Wisdom here is a veiled presentation of Christ Himself. Let us put Christ into the following verses and see what happens.

14. The benefit of knowing the Lord Jesus far surpasses any profit a man might get from silver and gold. He gives what money can never buy.

I'd rather have Jesus than silver or gold.
I'd rather be His than have riches untold,
I'd rather have Jesus than houses or land,
I'd rather be led by His nail-pierced hand
Than to be the king of a vast domain
And be held in sin's dread sway.
I'd rather have Jesus than anything
This world affords today.

George Beverly Shea

15. He is more precious than corals, rubies, or any other jewels, more to be desired than any earthly prize.

16. With one hand He offers long life, in fact, eternal life. With the other, spiritual wealth and honor.

17. All His ways are pleasant, and all His paths are peace. "Where He guides, journeying is pleasant, where He points the way, all is peace" (Knox, alt.).

18. To those who receive Him, He is like a tree whose fruit is life worth living. Those who remain close to Him are the happy ones.

19,20. These two verses describe the wisdom of God in creation, in judgment, and in providence. In creation He founded the earth and established the heavens. In judgment, He opened up the fountains of the great deep at the time of the Flood. In providence, He lifts the water from the ocean into the sky, then distributes it again as rain upon the earth.

And who is the active agent of the godhead in doing all this? It is Christ, the Wisdom of God (John 1:3; Col. 1:16; Heb. 1:2).

21. The privilege of being instructed by the Wisdom that created and sustains the universe is too great to miss. We shouldn't let sound wisdom and discretion out of our sight.

22. They provide inward vitality (life unto thy soul) and outward beauty (grace to thy neck).

23. They enable a man to walk with confidence, free from danger of tripping or slipping.

24. They guarantee a good night's sleep, with no guilt on the conscience and no fear on the mind.

25. They preserve a man from the kinds of calamity that overtake the wicked. Those who envy the apparent prosperity of the ungodly fail to realize the built-in hazards of that kind of life—such as extortion, theft, revenge, pay-offs, kidnapping, and murder.

26. The Lord guards those who walk in His ways. He won't let their feet get caught in traps. We are often conscious of God's marvelous interventions and rescues in our lives. But these are only the tip of the iceberg. Some day we will realize more fully all we have been saved *from* as well as saved *to*.

27. Notice the negatives in verses 27-31: "Withhold not . . . say not . . . devise not . . . strive not . . . envy not . . . choose not. . . ."

First, never withhold anything from its owner when you are in a position to give it. This might refer to wages that have been earned, to a debt that is due, to tools that have been borrowed.

But in a wider sense it may mean, "Never withhold a kindness or a good deed from someone who is entitled to it."

28. Don't put your neighbor off till tomorrow when you can meet his need today.

Who is my neighbor? Anyone who needs my help.

What does my neighbor need? He needs to hear the Good News of Salvation.

If the Holy Spirit burdens my heart to witness to someone, I should do it today. Never refuse any prompting of the Spirit.

29. Love to our neighbor forbids us to plot harm against him as he dwells trustingly and unsuspectingly in the house next door. This rules out all the mean, sarcastic, and cruel revenge that too often follows neighborhood squabbles.

30. Here we are warned against picking a fight with a man when he has done nothing to provoke it. There is already enough strife in the world without needlessly going around to stir up more.

31,32. The man of violence may seem to have instant success. But we should not envy his prosperity or follow his example. The Lord hates, loathes, despises, and abominates the perverse man, but He takes the upright into His intimate confidence (see John 14:23).

33. God's condemnation or His confidence, His curse or His blessing—that is the choice! A dark cloud hovers over the house of the wicked. The sunshine of God's favor beams down on the good man's house.

34. Again the choice is between God's scorn and His grace. He scorns the scoffer but gives grace to the humble. The importance of this choice is seen in that the verse is quoted twice in the New Testament (Jas. 4:6; 1 Pet. 5:5).

35. Finally the choice is between honor and disgrace. Wise men are honored, fools become well-known by falling into disgrace.

CHAPTER 4

1. In the first nine verses, Solomon rehearses the sound teaching which his father had passed on to him, and urges his sons to spare no effort in gaining true insight. The book of Proverbs teems with earnest exhortations to the young to listen to the instruction of a wise father.

2. It pays to cultivate the friendship of godly, older people. You can learn a lot from them and benefit from their years of experience. Their doctrine is good, and not to be disregarded.

3. Here Solomon reverts to the time when he was a son to his father and "the only son" (NASB) in the sight of his mother. Actually he was not an only son, but perhaps the expression means "my mother's darling" (Knox).

4. Solomon's father, David, had urged his son to follow his sound advice and thus live a life that counts. A summary of David's instruction is given in verses 4b-9.

5,6. His major concern was for his son to get wisdom and understanding—which really means to live for the Lord. Whatever else Solomon did, he should never forget this, because only the life that's lived for God really counts.

7. The first step in getting wisdom is to have motivation or determination. We get in life what we go after. We should get wisdom at all cost, and in the process get good insight and discernment. This means, among other things, that we will learn to choose between the evil and the good, the good and the best, the soulish and the spiritual, the temporal and the eternal.

8. If we give wisdom first place in our priorities, she will reward us handsomely. If we embrace her lovingly, she will promote us to places of honor.

9. "She will adorn you with charm and crown you with glory" (Moffatt). Wisdom confers a moral beauty on her children. Contrast, for instance, the repulsiveness of a life abandoned to dissipation and immorality.

10. Having finished quoting his father's counsel, Solomon now resumes his appeal to his own son. It is a general rule, though not without exceptions, that a clean life is conducive to a long life. Think how tobacco, alcohol, drugs, and sexual sin are directly linked with disease and death.

11. A father can be gratified when he has taught his son the ways of wisdom and has been a good example to him.

However, the teaching must be combined with the example. A father's actions speak louder than his words.

12. A son who walks in the right paths will walk unimpeded and will run without stumbling.

The Syriac version reads, "As thou goest step by step, I will open up the way before thee." This teaches two important principles: First, God guides us step by step, rather than revealing the whole plan at once. Second, God guides people when they are moving forward for Him. A ship must be in motion before the skipper can steer it. So must a bicycle; you can only guide it when it is moving. The same is true of us; God guides us when we are in motion for Him.

13. We should lay hold of good teaching, and not let it slip from us. We should guard wisdom as we would guard our life—because it is our life, especially when we think of Wisdom Incarnate in the person of the Lord Jesus.

14. Verses 14-19 warn against evil companions and contrast the way of darkness with the way of light.

These exhortations against joining up with unrighteous men do not forbid our witnessing to them but they do forbid any partnership in their plans.

15. There is a note of urgent warning in these short, staccato commands. Stay clear of a life of sin. Don't pass by to investigate. Turn the other way. Keep going. It might seem interesting, intriguing, and thrilling, but it eventually will destroy you.

16. The henchmen of sin can't sleep well unless they have pulled some shady deal. They get a king-sized case of insomnia unless they have lured someone to ruin and disaster.

17. Their diet is the bread of fraud and the wine of violence. Or we might say that wickedness is their meat and drink.

18. Not so the life of the righteous man. It is like the dawning light which increases in splendor until it reaches the full blaze of noonday. In other words, the path of the just grows better and brighter all the time.

19. The wicked stagger on in deep darkness, with no idea as to what they're stumbling over.

20. Solomon continues to plead with his son to pay close attention to his instruction in wisdom. In a verse like this, we should hear the voice of the Lord speaking to us.

21. It is for our own good that we should not let wisdom's teachings out of our sight, but should rather treasure them in our hearts.

22. Wisdom's words are life-giving and creative. As Jesus said, "The words that I speak unto you, they are spirit, and they are life" (John 6:63).

And they are health to the whole body because they deliver a person from the sins and stresses that cause so much illness.

23. Verses 23-27 are the Old Testament counterpart of Romans 12:1. They beseech us to present our entire beings to God—heart, mouth, lips, eyes, and feet. God begins with the inner man, then works outward.

The heart is first. It speaks of the inner life, the mind, the thoughts, the motives, the desires. The mind is the fountain from which the actions flow. If the fountain is pure, the stream that flows from it will be pure. As a man thinks, so is he. So this verse emphasizes the importance of a clean thought life.

24. A froward mouth signifies dishonest and devious speech. Perverse lips refer to conversation that is not straightforward and aboveboard.

25. Eyes and eyelids that look straight ahead suggest a walk with singleness of purpose, one that does not turn aside for sin or for anything that is unworthy. In a day when the mass media bombard us with publicity designed to arouse our animal appetites, we must learn to keep our eyes on Jesus (Heb. 12:2).

26. If we are careful to walk the highway of holiness, all our ways will be well ordered and safe.

27. All along the highway, to the right and to the left, there are bypaths which lead to the haunts of sin. "Let's be true to Jesus, though a thousand voices from the world may call."

When tempted to go to a questionable place, ask yourself, "Would I like to be found there when Jesus returns?"

CHAPTER 5

1,2. Solomon is anxious to warn his son against one of the besetting sins of youth. Those who listen to sound advice and learn from the experience of others develop true discernment. Because their speech is pure and true, it protects them from getting into trouble.

3. The rest of the chapter deals with what has been called "the oldest profession"—prostitution.

The strange woman is a prostitute, one who hires herself out for immoral purposes. She may be thought of as a symbol of sin, of the evil world, of false religion, of idolatry, or of any other seductive temptation that the sons of men meet.

Her lips drip honey—sweet, smooth, and specious. She is a flatterer. Butter would melt in her mouth. She is a slick, clever talker.

4. At first she seems pleasant and desirable, but in the end she is bitter as wormwood. It is the old story—sin is attractive as a prospect but hideous in retrospect.

The price of going to bed with her is enormous—guilty conscience, remorse, scandal, venereal disease, wrecked marriage, broken home, mental disturbance, and a host of other ills.

5. She leads her victims down a one-way street to death and the grave.

6. Abandoned woman, she cares nothing for the good life. Her character is unstable and shifty, and she doesn't realize how low she has fallen. "The high road of Life is not for her, shifty and slippery are her tracks" (Moffatt).

7. As he considers all that is at stake, Solomon injects a solemn warning to his son, to listen to and obey what he has to say.

8. One great safeguard is to stay as far away from the temptation as possible. There is no use asking God for deliverance if we insist on toying with objects or places that are associated with sin.

In some cases, it is necessary to actually flee. Joseph did this, and although he lost his coat, he maintained his purity and gained a crown.

In order to obey verse 8 we may have to get a new job, move to a different location, or take some other equally decided step.

9. Those who visit the brothel squander their manly vigor, and give the best of their golden years to a cruel temptress.

10. In addition, they often find themselves the victims of blackmail. If they don't pay "hush money," they are threatened with public exposure.

11. The end of such a life is punctuated with a protracted groan, as the body is racked with gonorrhea, syphilis, blindness, locomotor ataxia, or emotional disturbances.

12,13. There is the added grief of regret and remorse. The burned out wreck reproaches himself for not having listened to his parents, his Sunday School teacher, his Christian friends. He could have avoided oceans of misery, but he was too pig-headed to be warned.

14. And there is the possibility of being brought to public disgrace. That seems to be the thought in this verse, although it might also include the idea of being sentenced for his misdeeds.

15. In figurative language, Solomon counsels his son to find all his sexual satisfaction with his own wife in a life of pure married love.

16. If we follow the King James Version, this verse describes the blessings of a faithful marriage relationship reaching out to family and friends.

The New American Standard Bible changes the verse to a question: "Should your springs be dispersed abroad, streams of water in the streets?" This is a picturesque description of the utter waste of one's reproductive powers that is involved in going in to a prostitute.

Knox translates the verse, "Thence let thy offspring abound, like waters from thy own fountain flowing through the public streets." The wife here is the fountain, and the waters are the children, tearing out of the house and playing happily in the streets.

17. The true marriage relationship is an exclusive one, and the children enjoy the security of "belonging." So this verse warns against the tragedy of illegitimate children or the doubtful parentage of those who are born as a result of promiscuous sexual union.

18. The fountain here again refers to a man's own wife. Let him find his joy and companionship in the wife of his youth. In "forsaking all other" a man finds that "there is no end to the richness that springs out of that exclusive relationship, and the warmth of the welcome that reaches out from his home to bless others" (Michael Griffiths).

19. Let a man reserve the intimacies of marital union for his wife, treating her as the loving, gracious woman she is. Let her love be his satisfying portion. "Be exhilarated always with her love" (NASB).

20. Why should he be exhilarated by the false charms of an adulteress? Or why fold an adventuress into his arms?

21. Though no human eye may follow him to the brothel, yet God sees all that takes place. "Secret sin on earth is open scandal in heaven."

22. Man cannot sin and get away with it. Sin's built-in consequences are inescapable.

"Sinful habits are hard to break, but if they are not broken, they will bind the client ever more tightly. He is held fast by these ropes of his own sin. He finds that sin spirals in a downward cycle, pulling him along. He is captured and tied up by sin's ever-tightening cords. At length he becomes sin's slave" (Jay Adams).

23. Ellicott calls this verse the final scene in the life of the profligate. He would not exercise self-control. Now he dies as a result. "For lack of sense he dies; his utter folly ruins him" (Moffatt).

The poet Shelley is an illustration of this passage. In his conceit, he ridiculed the idea of monogamous marriage, as if it were a matter of marrying one and disappointing thousands. The results of his approach, according to Griffiths, were desertions, suicides, illegitimate children, and jealousy. G. Sampson questioned "whether in the life of any poet there is such a trail of disasters as that which this 'beautiful but ineffectual' angel left behind him."

Lesson Three
Proverbs 6,7

CHAPTER 6

1. The first five verses are a warning against suretyship, that is, making oneself liable for someone else's debt in case that other person is unable to pay. Suppose a neighbor wants to buy a car on the installment plan but doesn't have much of a credit rating. The loan company demands the signature of someone who can pay in case the borrower defaults. The neighbor comes to you and asks you to cosign the note with him. This means that you will pay if he doesn't.

The friend in this verse is your neighbor. The stranger is the loan company to which you give your guarantee.

2. Most modern translations preface this verse with *if:* "If you have been snared with the words of your mouth, have been caught with the words of your mouth." In other words, if you have made a rash promise, you have fallen into a trap. It was a great mistake.

3. Now the best thing to do is to get yourself released from the agreement. Try to persuade your neighbor to get your signature removed from the note you have been trapped into signing.

4,5. The matter is of such importance that you shouldn't rest until you are released from this liability. You should squirm free like a gazelle from its captor, or a bird from the fowler.

But why does the Bible warn against suretyship so sternly? Isn't it a kindness to do this for a friend or neighbor? It might seem to be a kindness, but it might not be at all.

1. You might be helping him to buy something which it is not God's will for him to have.

2. You might be encouraging him to be a spendthrift or even a gambler.

3. If he defaults and you have to pay for something that is not your own, friendship will end and bitterness begin.

It would be better to give money outright if there is a legitimate need. In any case, you should not become surety for him.

6. Verses 6-11 are a protest against laziness. The ant is an object lesson to us as it scurries back and forth, keeps on the move, and often carries oversized loads.

7. It gets a lot accomplished without benefit of a boss, foreman, or superintendent. When we watch a swarm of ants, they seem to move crazily in every direction, but their activity is purposeful and directed, even though there is no apparent chain of command.

8. This little creature diligently and industriously works in summer and in harvest. The emphasis here is not on making provision for the future but on hard work now.

This passage should not be used to teach that Christians should make provision for a rainy day. We are forbidden to lay up treasures on earth (Matt. 6:19). It is true that ants do provide for their future, and it is also true that Christians should provide for theirs. But the difference is that an ant's future is in this world, whereas the believer's future is in heaven. Wise Christians, therefore, lay up their treasures in heaven, not on earth.

9. The lazy fellow seems to have an endless capacity for sleep. His philosophy is, "It's nice to get up in the morning, but it's nicer to lie in your bed." He seems to have an infinite deafness to alarm clocks.

10. When finally roused, he says, "Just let me have a few more winks, a little more sleep, a short nap, a quick beauty rest."

11. The rest of the household may wait, but the day of poverty won't. "Your poverty will come in like a vagabond, and your need like an armed man" (NASB).

12. Verses 12-15 are a classic description of a con man. He is a malicious swindler whose cunning smile masks a treacherous heart. He goes around with falsehood on his lips.

13. He uses all kinds of suggestive gestures and sinister motions to signal to his accomplice or to take his victims off guard. He winks his eyes, shuffles or scrapes with his feet, and beckons with his fingers.

14. His heart is filled with malice and deceit as he incessantly plots mischief and sows discord.

15. "Such men will be overtaken by their doom ere long, crushed all of a sudden beyond hope of remedy" (Knox). If you look hard enough, you can probably find an illustration of this in today's newspaper.

16. The things which characterize this wicked man (vv. 12-15) are hated by God (vv. 16-19), especially the sowing of discord (compare vv. 14 and 19).

The formula "six things . . . yes, seven . . ." may mean that the list is suggestive but not exhaustive. Or it may indicate that the seventh is worst of all.

17. *A proud look.* Pride is dust deifying itself. The valet of an emperor said, "I cannot deny that my master was vain. He had to be the central figure in everything. If he went to a christening, he wanted to be the baby. If he went to a wedding, he wanted to be the bride. If he went to a funeral, he wanted to be the corpse."

A lying tongue. The tongue was created to glorify the Lord. To lie is to pervert its use for that which is ignoble.

Is it ever right for a believer to lie? The answer is that God cannot lie, and He cannot give the privilege to anyone else.

Hands that shed innocent blood. Every human life is of infinite value to God. He proved this by paying an infinite price at Calvary for our redemption.

The institution of capital punishment (Gen. 9:6) reflects God's attitude toward murder.

18. *A heart that deviseth wicked imaginations*. This, of course, refers to the mind that is always plotting some evil. The Lord Jesus listed some of these wicked imaginations in Mark 7:21,22.

Feet that be swift in running to mischief. God hates not only the mind that plans the evil but the feet that are eager to carry it out.

19. *A false witness that speaketh lies*. Here it is a matter of public testimony in a court of law. In verse 17b it was more a matter of everyday conversation.

He that soweth discord among brethren. The striking thing here is that God ranks the one who causes divisions among brethren with murderers, liars, and perjurers.

How many of the seven sins listed above can you associate with the trial and crucifixion of our Lord?

20. The subject of adultery or unfaithfulness is taken up again here. The frequency with which it recurs is not accidental.

The words of verse 20 are a sort of formula used to introduce important instruction.

21. Some extreme literalists in Jesus' day thought they obeyed this verse by wearing phylacteries, that is, small leather boxes containing Scripture portions. During prayer, these Jews wore one on the left arm (near the heart) and one on the head (near the neck).

But what this verse really means is that we should make the Word of God so much a part of our lives that it will accompany and direct us wherever we go. It is not just a question of honoring the Scriptures outwardly but of obeying them from the heart.

22. Obedience to God's Word affords:

guidance—when thou goest, it shall lead thee.

protection—when thou sleepest, it shall keep (guard) thee.

instruction—when thou awakest, it shall talk with thee.

23. This verse amplifies the previous one:
the commandment is a lamp—for guidance.
the law is light—for protection.
the reproofs of instruction are the way of life—for instruction.

24. One particular ministry of the Word is to save men from the adulteress with the glib, flattering tongue.

25. No one should be taken in by her natural beauty or by the come-hither flickers of her eyelashes.

26. The interpretation of this verse differs according to different translations.

The thought in the King James Version and the New American Standard Bible is that a man is brought to poverty by a harlot, and may lose his life to an adulteress. Both kinds of entanglement are costly.

The Revised Standard Version says, "for a harlot may be hired for a loaf of bread, but an adulteress stalks a man's very life." Here a distinction is made between a harlot, who can be hired, and an adulteress who is not satisfied until she controls the man completely.

27. To have illicit relations with another man's wife is like carrying fire in one's bosom. You can't do it without being burned.

28. It is like walking on hot coals; you can't do it without burning your feet. "It is utter folly for all that will commit adultery, for the result will be self-destruction, wounds and dishonor, disgrace, and the unappeased anger of the wronged parties" (Griffiths).

29. As sure as a man goes in to his neighbor's wife, he will be caught and punished. There is a principle in the moral universe by which such sin is generally brought to light. Even, if by some remote chance, his sin is not discovered in this life, it will have to be accounted for in the next.

30,31. These verses may be understood in one of two ways. According to the King James Version and the New American Standard Bible people have a measure of sympathy if a man steals to feed himself and his hungry family, but even then, if he is caught, he has to make restitution, even if it means losing everything he owns.

The Revised Standard Version, by changing verse 30 into a question, implies that men do despise a thief, even if he steals to satisfy his hunger, and that he has to make complete restitution.

In either case, the point is that a thief can make restitution for his crime whereas an adulterer can never fully erase the damage he incurs.

32. The one who commits adultery has no sense because he destroys himself socially, spiritually, and morally, and perhaps even physically (Deut. 22:22).

33. For one moment of passion, he gets wounds, perhaps from the enraged husband, and he gets shame and disgrace that will dog him the rest of his life. (Thank God, however, there is forgiveness with the Lord if the man will repent, confess, and forsake his sin.)

34. Here we see the fury of the jealous husband who returns unexpectedly and finds his wife in the arms of another man. When he starts to take revenge, he will not be conciliated by any pleas or excuses.

35. Nothing that the offender could pay would appease the husband; no bribe would be sufficient satisfaction for the violation of his marriage.

CHAPTER 7

1. This chapter continues to warn young people against ruining their lives by immorality. They should treasure these inspired instructions as more valuable than earthly, material riches.

2. Obedience to God's Word is the pathway to abundant living. Therefore, it should be kept as the apple of the eye. With regard to this expression, the International Standard Bible Encyclopedia says: "The eyeball, or globe of the eye, with pupil in center, is called 'apple' from its round shape. Its great value and careful protection by the eyelids' automatically closing when there is the least possibility of danger made it the emblem of that which was most precious and jealously protected."

3. In poetic language, this verse says to let the Word of God control all that we do (bind them upon thy fingers) and become a matter of unquestioning obedience (write them upon the table of thine heart).

4. We should treat Wisdom with the honor and respect due to a sister, and make understanding one of our intimate friends (see NASB). Wisdom in this passage is contrasted with the evil woman, who is to be carefully avoided.

5. Those who follow Wisdom and her instructions are preserved from the strange woman and from the flattery of the stranger. Two different words are used here to describe this evil woman. Strange means loose and faithless to her marriage vows. Stranger means foreigner and adventuress.

6. Verses 6-23 give a vivid account of a prostitute plying her trade and of a young man being "taken in" by her. The tragic drama unfolded as the writer was looking through the venetian blinds on his window.

7. An empty-headed, aimless young fellow is out on the town. Perhaps he is from a decent home, but now he is out to have a good time. It could be that he is a G.I. who isn't going to be outdone by his boasting pals. He isn't really a hardened sinner, just an inexperienced smalltown guy.

8. Now he wanders into the red-light district. He crosses the street near the house where she lives. He slowly saunters on with the gait of idleness. That's the whole trouble. If he were busy in some constructive, worthwhile activity, he wouldn't be here. If his feet were shod with the preparation of the gospel of peace, he wouldn't have time to waste! There is real protection from sin in a life sold out to God. On the other hand, "Satan finds some mischief still, for idle hands to do" (Isaac Watts).

9. He has been wandering around all evening—from sunset to dusk to midnight blackness. "There is a certain symbolic meaning in the picture of the gathering gloom. Night is falling over the young man's life as the shadows deepen" (Barnes).

He is like a moth flying to the flame. The awful moment of danger approaches when the temptation to sin and the opportunity to sin coincide. We should pray constantly that these two should never come together in our lives.

10. The prostitute now makes her appearance, dressed to kill in the latest Hollywood styles, painted, powdered, and perfumed. Beneath her charming exterior lies a sensuous, secretive, subtle heart.

11. No gracious, modest lady this! She is brash, loud, and aggressive. Not for her to be a homemaker! She must prowl the streets for clients.

12. She is almost ubiquitous. "Now in the street, now in the market, and at every corner she lies in wait" (RSV). Sin is like that; it is easy to find. The Gospel should be easy to find, but unfortunately we fail to make it widely available.

13. The first step in her technique is the shock treatment. She rushes up to him, throws her arms around him and kisses him. Wow! He is swept off his feet by this tremendous display of love. He doesn't know it is lust, not love.

14. Next comes the religious pose. She says, "I have peace offerings with me; this day have I paid my vows." He remembers his mother and the Bible on the living room table, then says to himself, "This woman must be all right. She's religious. I can't go wrong with anyone who has peace offerings and who pays her vows." The noose is tightening.

There is an added lure in the peace offerings. Those who offered them had to eat them that day or the next (Lev. 7:15 ff), so she has plenty of good food with which to regale him. She believes that at least one way to a man's heart is through his stomach.

15. Then she pretends that he is the one she has been looking for. What a lie! She would have taken the first man who came along. But he is elated to think that he is important; someone really appreciates him, someone really cares.

16,17. She gives more than a hint of her proposal by describing her bed: "I have decked my couch with coverings, colored spreads of Egyptian linen" (RSV). Everything here is designed to appeal to his sensual nature. Even his sense of smell is to be captivated by exotic perfumes.

18. Now the veil is torn away. She openly invites him to go to bed with her. With carefully chosen words, she makes it all sound very pleasurable.

19,20. She disarms him by explaining that the man of the house is not at home and won't be home for a long time, because he has gone on an extended journey. He expected to be away for a long time because he took a good supply of cash with him. He wouldn't come home till full moon (v. 20b NASB). The darkness described in verse 9 indicates that the moon wouldn't be full for some time.

21. The more she talks, the more his resistance melts. With a little more flattery, she coaxes him to yield.

22. He makes a snap decision to follow her to her house. "Straightway" in the AV is better translated "all at once."

As he saunters along with her, there is all the pathos of an ox going unwittingly to the slaughter.

The Hebrew text of the last line is very obscure, as will

be seen by the variety of translations.

"or as a fool to the correction of the stocks" (AV).

"or as a stag is caught fast" (RSV).

"like a dog cajoled to the muzzle" (Moffatt).

"or as a frisky lamb" (Knox).

"as in fetters a fool to his punishment" (Berkeley).

"or as one in fetters to the correction of the fool" (ASV).

But the general sense is clearly that the victim is moving irresistibly toward shackles and punishment.

23. The expression "till a dart strike through his liver" may mean:

1. the method by which the ox in the preceding verse is killed, i.e., a knife pierces its entrails.

2. the thorough inflaming of the man's passions.

3. the consequences of immorality in the man's body.

The young man goes in to the harlot like a bird flies into a net, little realizing what it is going to cost him.

24. No wonder then that the writer pleads for an attentive ear from his children.

25. They should guard their minds against any desire to associate with this type of woman. They should guard their feet from walking in her direction.

26. Her list of victims is a long one. She has ruined or slain a great army.

27. Anyone who enters her house is on the broad road to Sheol; he is marching down to the chambers of death.

Lesson Four
Proverbs 8,9

CHAPTER 8

1. This chapter is in contrast to the former. There the adulteress called out to the sons of men. Here Wisdom invites them to follow her, and gives strong reasons for doing so. A parallel passage in the New Testament is John 7:37 where Christ calls men to come to Him and drink.

2,3. These verses tell *where* Wisdom is found. The list of places indicates that she is readily available to the race of men in their daily travels.

4,5. She issues her call to all types of men, to those of distinction and those of inferior rank. She calls to the simple and the fools. She is "the would-be guide of Everyman" (Kidner).

6-9. The character of Wisdom's teaching is next described. She speaks excellent things, right things, truth, and righteousness. From her lips come no evil, twisted, or crooked things. Anyone who has a measure of discernment and understanding will find them straight and just.

10,11. The value of Wisdom's teaching is incomparable. It is to be desired above silver, gold, rubies, or anything else that men prize highly.

12,13. Wisdom lives in the same house with prudence. They go together, so that, if you have Wisdom, you also have insight. Wisdom gives knowledge and discretion for the management of the affairs of life.

There are other things that Wisdom (the fear of the Lord) does not live with. They are moral opposites, and she despises them, namely, all forms of evil, whether pride, arrogance, wicked behavior, or lying speech.

14-21. Some of the rewards or benefits of Wisdom are:
  Good advice (v. 14a)
  Sound judgment (v. 14b)
  Understanding (v. 14c)
  Moral strength to do what is right and to resist evil (v. 14d)
  Leadership ability (vv. 15a,16a)
  Judicial skill (vv. 15b,16b)
  Affection and companionship (see John 14:21) (v. 17a)
  Ready access to those who mean business (v. 17b)
  Lasting wealth coupled with honor and righteousness (v. 18)
  Character that is worth more than gold or silver (v. 19)
  Guidance in paths of righteousness and of justice, bringing wealth in abundance (vv. 20,21).

22-31. We have already mentioned that these passages dealing with Wisdom can be fittingly applied to the Lord Jesus, since the New Testament refers to Him as Wisdom (Matt. 11:19; Luke 11:49; 1 Cor. 1:24,30; Col. 2:3). Nowhere is the application more clear and beautiful than in the passage before us. The Christian Church has consistently regarded this paragraph as referring to the Lord Jesus Christ.

What then do we learn about Christ in "this noble specimen of sacred eloquence"?

His eternal generation (v. 22). "The Lord possessed me in the beginning of His way." We must not understand the word "possessed" as implying that Christ ever had a beginning. God never existed without the quality or attribute of wisdom, and neither did He ever exist without the Person of His Son. The meaning here is exactly the same as in John 1:1: "In the beginning . . . the Word was with God. . . ."

His appointment from eternity (v. 23). "Set up" means anointed or appointed. Long before creation took place, He was appointed to be the Messiah of Israel and the Savior of the world.

His pre-existence (vv. 24-26). The words "brought

forth" must not be taken to mean that He was ever created and thus had a beginning. They are poetic language describing the Son's eternal existence and His personality as being distinct from that of God the Father.

"The highest part" (v. 26b AV) should be "beginning."

His presence at creation (vv. 27-29). He was there when the heavens were stretched over the land and sea, when clouds were formed, and fountains and springs began gushing forth. He was there when the boundaries of the oceans were decided upon, the waves being commanded not to pass beyond the limits set. He was there when the earth was made, including the internal structure that supports the outer crust.

His activity in creation (v. 30a). Here we learn that the Lord Jesus was the active Agent in creation. The NASB correctly renders the first part of verse 30, "Then I was beside Him, as a master workman. . . ." This agrees, of course, with John 1:3; Colossians 1:16; and Hebrews 1:2.

His position of affection and delight before God (v. 30b). The eternal and infinite love of the Father for His Son increases the marvel that He would ever send that Son to die for sinners.

His personal delight before God (v. 30c). This magnifies the grace of our Lord Jesus Christ—that He would ever leave that scene of pure and perfect joy to come to this jungle of shame and sorrow and suffering.

His delight in the inhabited earth (v. 31a). It is amazing that out of all the vast universe, He should be especially interested in this speck of a planet.

His special delight in the sons of men (v. 31b). The final wonder is that He should set His affection upon the rebel race of men.

William Cowper left us this magnificent hymn based upon verses 22-31.

> Ere God had built the mountains,
>   Or raised the fruitful hills;
> Before He filled the fountains

> That feed the running rills;
> In Thee, from everlasting
> The wonderful I AM
> Found pleasures never wasting,
> And Wisdom is Thy Name.
>
> When like a tent to dwell in,
> He spread the skies abroad,
> And swathed about the swelling
> Of ocean's mighty flood,
> He wrought by weight and measure;
> And Thou wast with Him then:
> Thyself the Father's pleasure,
> And Thine, the sons of men.
>
> And could'st Thou be delighted
> With creatures such as we,
> Who, when we saw Thee, slighted
> And nailed Thee to a tree?
> Unfathomable wonder?
> And mystery divine?
> The voice that speaks in thunder
> Says, "Sinner, I am thine!"

32-36. This final paragraph sets forth the eternal issues involved in man's response to Wisdom's call. It pronounces a blessing on those who heed her instruction, walking in her ways (vv. 32,33). It promises happiness to those who wait ardently at her gate, who keep faithful vigil at her doors (v. 34). It holds out life and divine favor to those who find her, but personal loss and death to those who miss her (vv. 35,36).

Apply these last two verses to Christ. Whoever finds Him receives eternal life and stands in full favor with God (see John 8:51; 17:3; Eph. 1:6 AV; 1 John 5:12). But those who miss Him injure themselves (v. 36 RSV), and those who hate Him love death (cf. John 3:36b).

CHAPTER 9

1. Here Wisdom is seen building a palace and preparing a great feast for those who will answer her invitation. A feast is especially appropriate as a picture of the joy, fellowship and satisfaction which she provides for her guests.

Various interpretations have been given for the seven pillars. Some commentators refer us to Isaiah 11:2, the sevenfold gifts of the Holy Spirit which rested on the Messiah; but actually only six are clearly listed. An alternate interpretation is found in James 3:17 (NASB) where the wisdom from above is described as (1) pure, (2) peaceable, (3) gentle, (4) reasonable, (5) full of mercy and good fruits, (6) unwavering, and (7) without hypocrisy.

2. Food and wine are served in abundance. The table is richly spread.

3. The regal hostess sends forth servants to issue the invitation "from the tops of the heights of the city" (NASB).

4-6. The actual words of the invitation are given. It is issued to the simple, that is, to impressionable people who are prone to go astray and therefore need help and guidance. It is not issued to the wise because they are already inside the palace.

The menu includes the finest foods and the most exquisite wines, mixed by Wisdom herself.

Those who come are expected to part company with fools, and show that a moral change has taken place in their own lives.

7-9. The continuity here seems to be broken, but perhaps these verses explain either why the invitation is not sent to scorners, or why Wisdom's guests must forsake them.

If you rebuke a scorner, you get only abuse for it. If you rebuke a wicked man, he'll turn on you and assault you.

The way in which a man receives rebuke is an index of his character. A scoffer hates you, whereas a wise man will thank you. How do you react when parent, teacher, employer, or friend corrects you?

Instead of resenting criticism, a wise man takes it to heart and thus becomes wiser. A righteous man benefits by increasing his store of useful knowledge.

10. Once again we are reminded that the starting point for all true wisdom is in fearing the Lord. "To know the Deity is what knowledge means" (Moffatt). Because he knows the Holy, a true believer can see more on his knees than others can see on their tiptoes.

The Holy (plural) may be the plural of majesty, excellence, and comprehensiveness, or it may modify Elohim (understood), a plural form of a name of God.

11. Wisdom leads to multiplied days and increased years. It provides not only for long life, but for good and productive living, and then—beyond that—for the life that never ends.

12. It is for a man's own best advantage to be wise; he benefits himself more than anyone else. On the other hand, if he chooses to scorn, he will suffer the penalty of his choice, though others may be dragged in as well, of course. In the long run, he is the winner or loser.

13. Those who reject Wisdom's feast are prime prospects for Folly's fast. Notice the obvious contrast between Wisdom's elegant offer (vv. 1-6) and Folly's tawdry proposition (vv. 13-18).

The foolish woman is loudmouthed, empty-headed, and brazenfaced.

14. She sits outside her front door or on conspicuous heights of the city, not as a gracious lady, but as the shameless harlot she is.

15,16. She is out to seduce men who are easily led, simple fellows who have no sense.

17. Her line is, "Stolen water is sweet; and bread eaten in secret is pleasant" (NASB). Basically she means that illicit intercourse is attractive because it is forbidden and because there is the intrigue of secrecy about it.

When fallen human nature is forbidden to do a certain thing, that prohibition stirs up the desire to do it all the more (see Rom. 7:7,8). The harlot appeals to this depraved instinct in man. She invites the gullible and "easy touches" in for a visit.

18. But she doesn't tell them the other side of the story. Following the moment of pleasure and passion is the lifetime of remorse and the eternity of hell.

Lesson Five
Proverbs 10—12

CHAPTER 10

Up to this point in the book of Proverbs, there has been a definite continuity of thought and a connection between the verses. Subjects have been dealt with in paragraph form. From 10:1 through 22:16 we have a series of 375 proverbs, each distinct in itself. Most of them present contrasting statements, separated by the word "but." It is no coincidence that the numerical value of the letters of Solomon's name in Hebrew is 375, corresponding to the number of proverbs in this section entitled "The Proverbs of Solomon."

1. The behavior of a son has a direct effect on the emotional health of his parents. Every son may turn out to be a Paul or a Judas, with all that means by way of joy or grief.

2. Wealth obtained illegally doesn't last; it has a way of disappearing. And in the hour of death, it cannot win a moment's reprieve. Righteousness, on the other hand, delivers from death in at least two ways. It preserves a man from the perils of a sinful life, and, as the outward evidence of the new birth, it shows that he has eternal life.

3. It is a general rule that God will not let the righteous go hungry. David said, "I have been young, and now am old; yet have I not see the righteous forsaken, nor his seed begging bread" (Psa. 37:25). But it is equally true that the Lord "thwarts the craving of the wicked" (RSV). Just as they reach out to grasp satisfaction and fulfilment, it eludes them.

4. The lazy, careless person reaps poverty. The one who is diligent and aggressive succeeds.

5. Summertime is reaping time. It is senseless to go to all the labor of plowing, planting, and cultivating, only to sleep when the time comes to harvest the crop. Jesus says to all His disciples, "Lift up your eyes, and look on the fields; for they are white already to harvest" (John 4:35).

6. The law of harvest is that we reap what we sow. If we sow an upright life, we will receive the blessing of God and the praise of our fellow-men. If we sow the wild oats of sin, our mouth will be covered with violence. This is what happened to Haman: his mouth was covered and he was led out to a violent death (Esth. 7:8-10).

7. The fragrance of a holy life lingers long after the person is gone. The memory of the wicked evokes a stench, not a fragrance. Men still call their sons Paul—but not Judas!

8. A wise-hearted person receives commandments in the sense that he is willing to listen to sound advice. The loud-mouthed fool, because of his unwillingness to learn and obey, is hurled down to his ruin.

9. There is safety and security in an upright life, but the life that is built on deception will be found out and exposed.

10. The contrast in this verse is clearer if we follow the RSV: "He who winks the eye causes trouble, but he who boldly reproves makes peace." The winking eye indicates subterfuge and cunning. When this form of deceit is frankly rebuked, peace is exchanged for sorrow.

11. The mouth of a righteous man is a fountain flowing with words of edification, comfort, and counsel. The mouth of the wicked is silenced by his violence and malice.

12. A hateful spirit isn't satisfied to forgive and forget; it insists on raking up old grudges and quarrels. A heart of love draws a curtain of secrecy over the faults and failures of others. These faults and failures must, of course, be confessed and forsaken, but love does not gossip about them or keep the pot boiling.

13. The conversation of an intelligent man is helpful to others. A fool helps no one, but only succeeds in bringing punishment on himself.

14. A wise man values knowledge and keeps it in store for the appropriate moment. "He reserves what he has to say for the right time, place, and persons (cp. Matt. 7:6)" (Barnes). But you never know what a foolish blabbermouth will say next. He is always bringing trouble to others and to himself.

15. The rich get richer and the poor get poorer. Those who have money can make money. The poor man can't get started; his poverty is his undoing. The rich can buy quality merchandise that lasts longer. The poor buy worn-out, second hand things that keep them poor with repair bills. This is the way things are in life, but not the way they should be.

16. Wealth obtained by reputable employment is a blessing. Profit from dishonorable work leads to sin. Compare a Christian carpenter and a non-Christian bartender. The income of the carpenter represents positive, productive work and is used for beneficial purposes. The work of the barkeeper is destructive. The more he works, the more he sins. The more he sins, the more he makes.

17. The one who makes it a practice to listen to godly instruction stays on the right road. The one who turns his back on good advice goes astray himself and leads others astray.

18. This proverb contrasts the man who conceals his hatred by insincere words and the man who openly reveals it by slandering his neighbor. The first is a hypocrite, the second is a fool, and there is not much to choose between them.

19. The more we talk, the greater is the probability of saying something wrong. Compulsive talkers should beware! The lust for incessant conversation often leads to exaggeration, breaking of confidences, and associated sins. Trying to top someone else's joke often mushrooms into off-color stories.

The man who exercises self-control in his speech is wise. He saves himself from embarrassment, apologies, and outright sin.

20. What a good man says is a reflection of what he is. Because his character is sterling, so is his speech. Since the heart (or mind) of the wicked man is not worthwhile, neither is the conversation that flows from it.

21. Someone has aptly paraphrased this proverb, "Good feeds itself and others. Evil cannot keep itself alive."

The fool here is the stubborn, intractable person.

22. It is only the blessing of the Lord that truly enriches a life.

But is it true that He adds no sorrow with it? How does this reconcile with the fact that the most godly people pass through times of deep sorrow?

There are several possible explanations for this second part of the proverb:
(1) God doesn't send sorrow. All sorrow, sickness, and suffering come from Satan. God often permits them in the lives of His children but He is not the source.
(2) Sorrow is not an ingredient of God's blessing as it is of prosperity apart from God.
(3) Another possible translation is "and toil adds nothing to it" (margin of RV and RSV). Here the thought is that toil, apart from God, adds nothing to the blessing. Toil is good, but unless it is God-directed, it is futile (see Psa. 127:1,2).

23. A fool amuses himself by getting into trouble; it's his favorite pastime. A man of understanding gets his pleasure in conducting himself wisely (see RSV).

24. The calamity which the wrongdoer fears will descend on him. The desire of the righteous—the will of God in this life and the presence of God in the next—will be granted. In this vein, C. S. Lewis said, "In the end, that Face which is the delight or the terror of the universe must be turned upon each of us either with one expression or the other, either conferring glory inexpressible or inflicting shame that can never be cured or disguised.''

25. When the storm of God's judgment passes, the transgressor is nowhere to be found. But the upright person is established on the Rock of Ages; nothing can ever move him.

26. Vinegar sets the teeth on edge, and smoke irritates the eyes. In the same way, a lazy messenger who dillydallies on the way proves exasperating, frustrating, and annoying to the one who sends him.

27. A devout life leads to longevity. Wicked men are cut off prematurely, e.g., gangland slayings, reprisal killings, deaths caused by drunkenness, drugs, and dissipation.

28. The things the righteous look forward to will be realized with rejoicing. Not so the wicked—their hopes will be thoroughly disappointed. ''Alexander the Great was not satisfied, even when he had completely subdued the nations. He wept because there were no more worlds to conquer, and he died at an early age in a state of debauchery. Hannibal, who filled three bushels with the gold rings taken from the knights he had slaughtered, committed suicide by swallowing poison. Few noted his passing, and he left this earth completely unmourned. Julius Caesar, 'dyeing his garments in the blood of one million of his foes,' conquered 800 cities, only to be stabbed by his best friends at the scene of his greatest triumph. Napoleon, the feared conqueror, after being the scourge of Europe, spent his last years in banishment'' (G. S. Bowes). Surely the expectation of the wicked perishes.

29. In His providential dealings the Lord proves to be a tower of strength to the man whose way is right, but destruction to evildoers.

30. God guarantees a dwelling place to the righteous, but the wicked shall be exiles and vagabonds.

The captivity of Israel illustrates this.

31. A good man's mouth is like a tree that brings forth blossoms of wisdom. The man whose speech is crooked and perverse is like a tree that will be felled.

32. You can depend on a good man to say the proper thing. The wicked man knows only how to distort the facts and to speak unpleasantly.

CHAPTER 11

1. Crooked merchants sometimes had two sets of weights, one for buying and one for selling. The buying weights were heavier than they should have been, so that he got more merchandise than he paid for. The selling weights were lighter than the standard, so that the customer got less than he paid for.

Do you know of any dishonest practices in business today that could be called a false balance?

How might this verse apply to school life, social life, home life, church life?

2. First, pride; then a fall; then shame connected with the fall.

Better to be humble and down-to-earth. This reduces the danger of tumbling.

3. Honesty is the best policy. The honesty of upright men keeps them on the right track; the experience of Joseph is an example. The crookedness of transgressors is their downfall; Balaam's life testifies to this.

4. Riches cannot avert the wrath of God in time or in eternity. Righteousness is a safeguard against premature death in the here and now. And only those who are clothed in the righteousness of God will escape the second death.

5. The upright man is directed by righteousness, the ideal guide. The wicked man stumbles, a victim of his own crookedness.

6. Righteousness not only guides the good man; it delivers him from perils seen and unseen. Apostates, like Judas, are caught in the meshes of their own lust and greed.

7. It has been said that a fool is a man, all of whose plans end at the grave. When the coffin lid closes, all his hopes are ended. The things he lived for are no longer his, and his expectation of prosperity is gone forever.

8. God delivers the righteous from calamity and sends it upon the wicked instead. Thus the three Hebrews were delivered out of the fiery furnace, but their would-be executioners were consumed by the fire (Dan. 3:22-26).

9. An apostate or godless man (NASB) seeks to undermine the faith of his neighbors with doubts and denials. Knowledge of the truth enables a man to detect the counterfeit, and to save himself and others from subversion.

10. Two occasions when a city breaks out in joyful celebration are when good men prosper and when the wicked die.

11. The blessing of the upright may refer to their prayers for the city (1 Tim. 2:1,2), or to the benefits which their presence and godly influence bring to the city (cp. Jesus' description of His followers as the salt of the earth in Matthew 5:13).

The deceit, broken promises, fraud, and profanity of the wicked are enough to ruin any local government.

12. "He who belittles his neighbor lacks sense, but a man of understanding remains silent" (RSV). To belittle another man is to insult God, to hurt the man, to invite strife, and to help no one. A wise man knows that it is better to say nothing if he can't praise or edify.

13. A gossip seems to take a malicious delight in spreading scandal, informing on others, and breaking confidences. He doesn't hold anything back, but tells everything he knows.

A faithful friend knows how to maintain a confidence and to refrain from talking.

14. Without wise leadership and statesmanship, the citizenry is bound to fall into trouble. On the other hand, there is safety in having the combined judgment of many good advisors.

15. To be surety for a stranger means to guarantee his debt or his promissory note. The person who does this will smart for it, that is, he will pay a stinging penalty. The man who avoids suretyship saves himself a lot of headaches. See notes on 6:1-5.

16. A gracious woman wins respect and honor, as is seen in the case of Abigail (1 Sam. 25). Violent men may gain money but they never get a good name.

17. A man's disposition affects his own health. The kind man avoids the dyspepsia, apoplexy, gastrointestinal ulcers, and heart trouble which the cruel man brings on himself.

The British Medical Journal once said that there is not a tissue in the human body that is wholly removed from the spirit. A cruel disposition takes its toll on the body.

18. "The wicked earns deceptive wages, but he who sows righteousness gets a true reward" (NASB). It is true that wicked men often seem to grow rich overnight, but their wealth is unsatisfying, unenduring, and unable to help them when they need it most. The rewards of a righteous life are real and permanent.

19. All conduct leads in one of two directions—either to life or to death. This proverb does not teach salvation by good works, however. No one can be "steadfast in righteousness" (NASB) unless he is in right relationship to God. He must first have been born again. A man who pursues evil proves thereby that he never was converted.

20. As far as God is concerned, a heart that is false is hateful and loathesome. He really likes the person who is straightforward.

No view of God is complete unless it sees that He is capable of hatred as well as of love.

21. "Though hand join in hand" means "assuredly" (NASB). Two things are certain in this uncertain world—the punishment of the wicked and the deliverance of the generation (seed) of the righteous.

22. A ring of gold in a pig's snout is incongruous. The snout is as unattractive as the ring is lovely. A beautiful woman who lacks discretion also combines two opposites—physical attractiveness and moral deficiency.

23. Righteous people aspire only for good and they get it. The wicked seek for evil and they get it in the form of wrath or judgment.

This proverb emphasizes the importance of having worthy goals, because ultimately we get what we go after in life. That is why Emerson said, "Hitch your wagon to a star." A British statesman urged his cabinet, "Whatever else you do, buy big maps."

24. Here is a glorious paradox. We enrich ourselves by being generous. We impoverish ourselves by laying up treasures on earth.

What we save, we lose.

What we give, we have.

Jim Elliott said, "He is no fool who gives what he cannot keep to gain what he cannot lose." And Dr. Barnhouse observed that everybody tithes, either to the Lord or to the doctor, the dentist, the garage mechanic.

25. The liberal person reaps dividends that the miser can never know. Whatever we do for others returns to us in blessing.

When a Sunday school teacher prepares diligently and then teaches her class, who do you think benefits from it most—the students or herself?

26. This man is keeping his corn off the market in a time of famine, hoping for greater return as the price is forced up. He is a profiteer, enriching himself by impoverishing and starving others. No wonder the people curse him. They want someone who will meet their desperate need now.

The world is perishing for the bread of life. The bread is free, and always will be. We have it to share with others. What are we waiting for?

27. When a man's motives are pure and unselfish, he wins the esteem of others. But the man who is out to cause trouble for others will get it for himself.

28. The New Testament counterpart of this proverb is 1 Timothy 6:17-19. Riches are uncertain and therefore not worthy of trust. Our confidence should be in the living God who gives us richly all things to enjoy.

"The lust of gold, unfeeling and remorseless, is the last corruption of degenerate man" (Samuel Johnson).

The righteous, that is, those whose trust is in the Lord, will flourish with life and vitality.

29. There are several types of men who trouble their own house—the drunkard, the crank, and the adulterer, for instance. But here it is probably the man who is greedy of gain (see 15:27), and who loses sight of the worthwhile values of life in his mad quest for wealth. He will inherit the wind, that is, end up with nothing tangible to satisfy his greed. His penalty for thus playing the fool will be servitude to a man who acts more wisely.

30. A righteous life is like a fruit-bearing tree that brings nourishment and refreshment to others. The wise man wins others to a life of wisdom and righteousness.

This is one of the great texts for soul winners in the Bible. It reminds us of the promise which Jesus made to Peter, "Thou shalt catch men" (Luke 5:10). What an unspeakable privilege it is to be used of God in doing a work in human lives that will result in eternal blessing! Every soul won to the Lord will be a worshiper of the Lamb of God forever and ever!

31. Even righteous people are chastised in this life for their misdeeds. Moses was excluded from the Promised Land and David had to restore fourfold. If the righteous reap what they sow, how much more do the ungodly. Or, as Peter put it, "if the righteous scarcely be saved, where shall the ungodly and the sinner appear?" (1 Pet. 4:18).

CHAPTER 12

1. Anyone who is open to correction and discipline shows that he really wants to learn. The man who resents being told anything and refuses correction is as stupid as a cow.

2. A moral, ethical man can be sure of the Lord's favor. A corrupt man can be equally sure of His judgment. "Think— the supreme Power in the universe against what a wicked man is doing, determined that he shall fail! The supreme Power leaving man to himself in silent scorn" (Foreman).

3. Lives that are dominated by sin have no stability. They are like the seed which fell upon the rocky places (Matt. 13:5,6); the earth was shallow and because they had no root, they quickly withered away.

A righteous man has his roots deep in God. He is able to stand when the storms of life blow. This man is described in Psalm 1:3.

4. A woman of quality brings joy and gladness to her husband. The one who disgraces her husband gives him a terrible letdown—as if his bones rotted away.

5. The goals of the righteous are honorable, and, just as surely, the plans of the wicked are treacherous. In other words, a man's aims are a mirror of his character.

6. By their speech sinners seek to lay fatal traps for the innocent and unwary. Upright men deliver themselves and others by speaking the truth.

7. When justice catches up with the wicked, that's the end of them. Godly people have a good foundation; they are not swept away by calamity.

8. People speak well of a man who has insight and who acts wisely, but they have nothing but contempt for one who has no principles.

9. "Better is a man of humble standing who works for himself than one who plays the great man but lacks bread" (RSV). The combination of low rank and food on the table is better than pretended status with starvation.

10. A good man's kindness extends even to dumb animals, but a wicked man is cruel, even when he thinks he is being most gentle.

Although God is transcendent, He is not too high to care for animals, but legislates concerning them (Exod. 20:10; 23:4,5). He even legislates concerning a bird's nest (Deut. 22:6).

11. A man who engages in positive, constructive work, like farming, will have his needs supplied. But with the man who spends his time in worthless pursuits, it's a matter not only of an empty cupboard but of an empty head.

12. The net of evil means, by metonymy, what is caught in the net of evil, or what is taken from others unjustly. In other words, the wicked want what belongs to others.

In contrast, the righteous are satisfied to provide quietly for their own needs.

13. Ungodly men are often trapped by their own words. By failing to tell a consistent story, they trip themselves up. A liar has to have a good memory; otherwise his accounts won't jibe. And to support a lie, he has to build a structure of other lies.

The man who is honest and guarded in speech avoids these problems.

Jesus taught His disciples "that every idle word that men shall speak, they shall give account thereof in the day of judgment. For by thy words thou shalt be justified, and by thy words thou shalt be condemned" (Matt. 12:36,37).

14. Good speech and good behavior carry their own reward with them. Wise, gentle, pure speech is rewarded with love, favor, and respect. Good deeds come back to a man in blessing.

15. You can't tell a fool anything. He knows everything and will not listen. "My mind is made up," he says, "don't confuse me with the facts." But a wise man will welcome advice. He recognizes that he doesn't know all the answers, and that others can help him see pros and cons that he had not considered.

16. It doesn't take long for a fool's anger to explode. He blows up at the slightest provocation. A prudent man knows how to ignore an insult (RSV) and to exercise self-control.

17. A true witness furthers the cause of justice, but a false witness hinders the truth from coming out and promotes deceit.

18. Some people use their tongue like a sharp sword, cutting, slashing, slicing. Others speak words of health and healing.

19. The man who consistently speaks the truth lays a solid foundation for this life and the next. He is established in God's favor and man's. The chronic liar is eventually exposed. Truth is eternal but "no lie reaches old age" (Sophocles).

20. Those who counsel others in the way of deceit become self-deluded; they believe their own falsehoods. Those who promote peace experience a deep-settled joy in their own hearts.

21. It is true in a general sense that no evil happens to the just. However, this is not a rule without exception. What is true without exception is that the just are preserved from the evil consequences that follow wicked behavior.

The wicked get plenty of this type of trouble.

22. God hates liars. How careful we should be about shading of the truth, white lies, exaggerations, and half-truths! A sure way of bringing joy to His heart is by being absolutely honest and trustworthy.

23. A true gentleman doesn't go around showing off how much he knows. He modestly conceals his learning. But you aren't long in the presence of fools before they reveal their empty-headedness.

24. In the ordinary course of life, industrious, dedicated people rise to positions of leadership just as cream rises to the surface. Laziness leads to poverty, and poverty reduces man to the level of slavery.

Oswald Chambers said that slovenliness is an insult to the Holy Spirit; he could have said the same thing about laziness.

25. Anxiety (NASB) causes a man's spirit to droop. A kind, encouraging, or sympathetic word works wonders in perking him up again.

26. Contrary to appearances, the righteous man is actually better off than his unrighteous neighbor. It doesn't seem that way. The sinner seems to have everything going his own way, and this seduces people into believing that forbidden fruit really is sweeter.

27. This lazy loafer either doesn't hunt (Moffatt, RSV) or he does not roast what he has taken in hunting (AV, NASB). In the first place he lacks the inertia to get started; in the second, he lacks the drive to finish what he began.

The Hebrew of the latter part of the proverb is also obscure, like the first part, but the sense almost surely is that a diligent person values what he has worked for and uses it to the best advantage. Ruth was like that; she beat out what she had gleaned (Ruth 2:17). In our Bible study, we should improve on what we have learned and we can do it through meditation, prayer, and practical obedience.

> Thus on Thy Holy Word we'd feed and live and grow,
> Go on to know the Lord, and practice what we know.

28. In the narrow path of holiness, there is life along the way and life at the close of the journey. There is no death in it, as there is on the broad road that leads to destruction (Matt. 7:13). "Life" here looks to a future beyond death, to eternal life. The NIV translates the verse, "In the way of righteousness there is life; along that path is immortality."

Lesson Six
Proverbs 13—15

CHAPTER 13

1. Both in physical and spiritual development, there is a normal process of development. A baby, for instance, must crawl before he walks or talks. In the spiritual realm, a convert must listen and learn before he launches forth in service. A wise son submits to the discipline of instruction. The scorner won't have it; he thinks he has all the answers, and refuses to be corrected.

2. Here is a man whose speech is edifying, encouraging, and comforting; he himself is rewarded when he sees the beneficial results of the spoken word. By way of contrast, the treacherous man plans violence for others, and he is paid in his own coin.

3. The man who guards his speech controls his whole life (see James 3:2b). The one who exercises no self-control is in for trouble. The lesson is: be careful what you say, it might be used against you.

4. "If wishes were horses, beggars would ride." The lazy man has great desires, but that isn't enough. "The wish without the exertion is useless." The diligent man applies himself to his work and carries home the bacon. This is true in spiritual matters as well as in temporal.

"Adam Clark is reported to have spent 40 years writing his commentary on the Scriptures. Noah Webster labored 36 years forming his dictionary; in fact, he crossed the ocean twice to gather material needed to make the book absolutely accurate. Milton rose at 4 o'clock every morning in order to have sufficient hours to compose and rewrite his poetry which stands among the best of the world's literature. Gibbon spent 26 years on his book *The Decline and*

Fall of the Roman Empire, but it towers as a monument to careful research and untiring dedication to his task. Bryant rewrote one of his poetic masterpieces 100 times before publication, just to attain complete beauty and perfection of expression. These men enjoyed what they were doing, and each one threw all of his energy into his effort no matter how difficult the job.

"The most happy and productive people are those who are diligent in their labors for the betterment of mankind and the glory of God" (Bosch).

5. A righteous man avoids any kind of dishonesty, but a wicked man "acts shamefully and disgracefully" (RSV).

"It is said of Abraham Lincoln that he would accept no case in which the client did not have justice on his side. One time a man came to employ him. Lincoln stared at the ceiling, yet listened intently as the facts were given. Abruptly, he swung around in his chair.

" 'You have a pretty good case in technical law,' he said, 'but a pretty bad one in equity and justice. You will have to get someone else to win the case for you. I could not do it. All the time while pleading before the jury, I'd be thinking, Lincoln, you're a liar! I might forget myself and say it out loud.'

"Lying and all forms of guilt grieve the heart of God. No Christian should lie or deceive, regardless of consequences to himself. If he does, he will never advance in the things of God" (J. Allen Blair).

6. A righteous life is a protected life. God undertakes to guard the upright. But the wicked walk in constant peril.

7. There are two ways of looking at this proverb. First, a man who has nothing in the way of material possessions may try to create the impression that he is wealthy, while one who actually has lots of money may give the appearance of being poor.

Or it may mean this. The godless millionaire actually is a spiritual pauper, whereas the humblest believer, though financially poor, is an heir of God and a joint heir with Jesus Christ.

"Our age abounds with men who have made themselves rich, and yet have nothing. They have amassed great wealth, and yet it has no purchasing power in the true things of life. It cannot insure health, it brings no happiness, it often destroys peace. On the other hand, there are those who have impoverished themselves, and have by so doing become wealthy in all the highest senses of the word. How is this to be explained? Is not the solution found by laying the emphasis in each of the contrastive declarations, upon the word *self*? To make *self* rich, is to destroy the capacity for life. To make *self* poor, by enriching others is to live. It is impossible to consider this saying of Hebrew wisdom, without thinking of the One who became incarnate Wisdom" (G. C. Morgan).

8. A rich man is often threatened by those who want his money. He faces robbery, blackmail, and kidnaping for ransom, and he has to guard his life by hiring protection or by meeting extortionate demands. The poor man never has to listen to this kind of threat (rebuke).

9. The testimony of the righteous is like a light that burns brightly and cheerily. The life and hopes of the wicked are a lamp that will go out.

10. There may be two thoughts in the first line. One is that when contentions come, pride is the invariable cause. Or second, "by pride there only cometh contention" (JND), that is, nothing good ever comes from pride: only bitter feuding. "It is Pride which has been the chief cause of misery in every nation and every family since the world began. Other vices may sometimes bring people together; you may find good fellowship and jokes and friendliness among drunken people or unchaste people. But Pride always means enmity—it *is* enmity. And not only enmity between man and man, but enmity to God" (C. S. Lewis).

Those who are willing to listen to good advice are wise; they avoid pride and the personality conflicts that go with it.

11. Wealth gotten by vanity means riches gained dishonestly, in haste or without exertion. This would include the money won by gambling, sweepstakes, or stockmarket speculation. This kind of wealth has a way of leaking out of a man's hands.

Wealth gained by honest, hard work accumulates instead of dwindling.

12. Repeated postponement of one's expectations is disheartening; but when the desire is at last fulfilled, it is a source of tremendous satisfaction. Apply this to the coming of the Lord.

13. The "word" here is the Word of God. Our attitude toward it is a matter of life and death. Those who despise it push the self-destruct button. Those who trust and obey are abundantly rewarded.

14. The counsel and instruction of wise men are a source of life and refreshment to those who heed. They deliver a person from fatal traps along life's pathway.

15. Good sense brings a person into favor with God and man. "A man with good sense is appreciated" (LB).

In the second part of the proverb, the word "transgressors" should be "treacherous" or "faithless." The word translated "hard" basically means permanent, enduring, or perennial. But to make good sense it has been taken to mean hard or rugged. If it meant permanent, there would have to be a negative, that is, "the way of the treacherous is *not* permanent." Perhaps we are best to stick to the traditional text: "the way of the treacherous is *hard*" (NASB). Every day's newspaper provides illustrations of that truth!

16. A man's conduct reveals his character. If a man is prudent, it comes out in the responsible way he acts. A fool puts his folly on display for everyone to see.

17. An unreliable messenger brings trouble to everyone concerned. Better to send a faithful man; he accomplishes his mission to the satisfaction of all.

"Now then we are ambassadors for Christ . . ." (2 Cor. 5:20).

18. "What simpletons acquire is folly: shrewd men will pick up knowledge" (Moffatt).

19. In order to make the contrast in this proverb complete, certain ideas must be supplied. The desire of the upright for happiness is accomplished by their departing from evil, and when it is realized, it is sweet to their soul. Fools also desire happiness, but they are unwilling to depart from evil, so they never taste the sweetness of realized desire.

20. It is good policy to cultivate the friendship of wise men; we can learn a lot from them. Folly rubs off on those who walk with fools, and they share a fool's end.

21. The sinner is dogged by the hounds of misfortune, physical harm, bad reputation, loss of possessions. The righteous enjoys a good reputation, a good life, and a good reward.

22. A good man leaves an inheritance not only to his children but to his grandchildren. In the Old Testament, this probably meant that he left material wealth for them. But a Christian today is better advised to leave a rich spiritual inheritance to his descendants.

The wealth of the sinner is laid up for the just; "ill-gotten gain has a way of finding better hands."

23. "Abundant food is in the fallow ground of the poor, but it is swept away by injustice" (NASB). There is great potential in the untilled land of the poor. However, it is often unrealized because the poor are oppressed by richer landlords. Or the meaning might be that the land doesn't produce abundant crops because of mismanagement or lack of discretion. Thus Darby translates the second line, "but there is that is lost for want of judgment."

24. To withhold punishment from a child when he deserves it is to weaken his own sense of security, to encourage him in sin, and to contribute to his eventual ruin. The parent might call this love, but God calls it hatred.

The parent who genuinely loves his child will not condone naughtiness or rebellion but will discipline the child promptly, consistently, and in love. The Bible teaches corporal punishment.

For many years, American parents raised their children according to the permissive teachings of the book *Baby and Child Care* by Dr. Benjamin Spock. These teachings were contrary to what we find here and elsewhere in the Scriptures. Later in life, Dr. Spock said that he had to share part of the blame for the "brattiness of many of today's children." He said, "Inability to be firm is . . . the commonest problem of parents in America . . . parental submissiveness doesn't avoid unpleasantness; it makes it inevitable."

25. God insures that the needs of the righteous will be supplied, but wicked men are equally assured of an empty stomach.

CHAPTER 14

1. A sensible housewife attends to her home and her family. The foolish woman goes gallivanting off to card parties, bingo games, fashion shows, and other empty amusements. She neglects her husband and children, and wonders why her family goes to ruin.

Is it possible for a woman to pluck down her house by too much religious activity too?

2. A man's conduct is a reflection of his attitude toward the Lord. The righteous man is guided by what he knows will please God. The crooked man doesn't care what God thinks, and thus reveals his contempt of Him. "Every departure from God's path is a pitting of one's will, and a backing of one's judgment, against His; but the contempt which it spills is too irrational to acknowledge" (Kidner).

3. "In the mouth of the foolish man lies a rod for his pride" (Berkeley). He will have to take a beating for his arrogant talk. The wise man's speech saves him from any such punishment.

4. A barn can be kept cleanly swept where there are no oxen, but isn't it better to have some dust and dirt around, knowing that the labor of the oxen will lead to a bountiful harvest? The rewards of toil more than compensate for its disagreeable aspects.

This proverb is not intended to encourage homes or chapels that look like disaster areas. But it does discourage that passion for order and dustlessness that puts the brakes on progress and productiveness.

5. C. H. Mackintosh once said that it is better to go to heaven with a good conscience than stay on earth with a bad one. How careful we should be to be utterly truthful at all times!

6. By continued refusal to listen, a scorner loses the capacity to hear. He can never find true wisdom as long as he rejects the Lord.

The man of understanding perceives the right thing quickly. "For whosoever hath, to him shall be given, and he shall have more abundance . . ." (Matt. 13:12).

7. Don't cultivate the friendship of a foolish man, "for there you do not meet words of knowledge" (RSV), or "you will not find a word of sense in him" (Moffatt).

8. For a prudent man wisdom means knowing how to behave honestly, conscientiously, and obediently. What a fool considers to be wisdom is actually folly, and the essence of that folly is deceiving others, which eventually results in self-deceit.

9. Although the Hebrew here is obscure, the AV makes good sense.

Fools make a mock of sin, will not believe;
It has a fearful dagger up its sleeve;

> "How can it be," they say, "that such a thing,
> So full of sweetness, e'er should wear a sting?"
> They know not that it is the very spell
> Of sin, to make them laugh themselves to hell.
> Look to thyself then, deal with sin no more.
> Lest He who saves, against thee shuts the door.
>
> Bunyan.

"Among the righteous there is favor." They enjoy the Lord's favor, free from the guilt and condemnation of sin.

10. There are sorrows in the human heart that no other human being can share (though the Lord can and does). There are also joys that can be enjoyed only by the person directly involved.

11. Notice the contrast between house and tent (tabernacle). We think of a house as permanent and a tent as temporary. But it is the tent of the upright pilgrim that survives, while the house of the wicked earthdweller tumbles.

12. The way which seems right to men is salvation by good works or good character. More people go down to hell laboring under that misconception than under any other. (See also 16:25.)

In a broader sense, the way which seems right to a man is his own way, the path of self-will that scorns divine guidance or human counsel. It can end only in disaster.

13. There is no such thing in life as pure, unadulterated joy. Sorrow is always mixed to some extent. Knox says, "Joy blends with grief, and laughter marches with tears."

14. "The backslider in heart will have his fill of his own ways, but a good man will be satisfied with his" (NASB). A person who wanders away from the Lord reaps the consequences of his waywardness. Thus Naomi said, "The Almighty hath dealt very bitterly with me. I went out full, and the Lord hath brought me home again empty" (Ruth 1:20b,21a). And the prodigal son said, "How many hired servants of my father's have bread enough and to spare, and

I perish with hunger!'' (Luke 15:17).

The upright man is satisfied with his ways, because they are the Lord's ways. He can say with David, "My cup runneth over" (Psa. 23:5c). Or with Paul, "I have fought a good fight, I have finished my course, I have kept the faith" (2 Tim. 4:7).

15. A naive, gullible person is susceptible to every new idea or fad. The prudent man takes a second look and thus preserves himself from error. Faith demands the surest evidence, and finds it in the Word of God. Credulity believes what every passing scientist, philosopher, or psychologist has to say.

16. A wise man fears in the sense that he is careful and cautious. Of course, the verse may also mean that he fears the Lord.

The fool is arrogant and careless (NASB), throws off restraint (RSV), and is obviously overconfident.

17. A man of quick temper acts foolishly. In anger, he does things without stopping to consider the consequences. He slams doors, throws whatever is handy, yells curses and insults, breaks furniture, and walks out in a rage. But if we had to choose, we could tolerate him more easily than the man of wicked devices. Everyone hates this man for his cold-blooded treachery.

18. "The simple acquire folly" (RSV). If they refuse to listen to sound teaching, they thereby choose to become more stupid.

The prudent are honored and rewarded by acquiring more and more knowledge.

19. This proverb points to the eventual triumph of good over evil. God will vindicate the cause of the righteous. The day came when Haman had to bow before Mordecai. And the day will come when every knee in the universe will bow before Jesus Christ as King of kings and Lord of lords.

20. "The poor is hated even by his neighbor" (NASB). It

shouldn't be this way, but it often is. Many people form friendships on the basis of self-interest. They avoid the poor and cultivate the rich for selfish ends. We should be interested in people for what we can do for them, not what we can get from them.

In one sense the rich man has many friends, but in another sense he never knows how many true friends he has, that is, friends who love him for who he is rather than for what he has.

21. This verse is obviously connected with the preceding one. It is sin to despise the poor because God has chosen them (Jas. 2:5). The man who has compassion on the poor is blessed in the act.

We should never forget that the Lord Jesus came into the world as a poor man. Someone referred to Him as "my penniless friend from Nazareth."

22. Those who plot mischief and devise evil plans are destined to go astray. Those who work for the good of others are rewarded with mercy and truth. This means that God shows kindness to them and is true to His promises of protection and reward. It also means that men repay them with loyalty and faithfulness (RSV).

23. Every kind of honorable work is profitable. Nothing but talk leads to nothing but poverty. We all know people who talk by the hour about their problems but never lift a little finger to solve them. They talk up a storm about world evangelism but never move from their Lazy-Boy reclining chair to witness to their neighbor. They tell you what they plan to do in the future (without coming up for air), but they never do it.

24. The glory of a wise man is his wealth; he has something to show for his wisdom, whether we think of that wealth as spiritual or material. Fools have nothing but folly to show for their lives and labors.

25. A true witness in a court of law delivers innocent people from being "framed." A false witness misrepresents the facts, with all the ruinous results that flow from such deceit.

The gospel preacher is a true witness who delivers souls from eternal death. The "modernists" and "cultists" are deceitful witnesses who speak lies and lead souls astray.

26. The man who fears the Lord has every reason to be confident. If God is for him, no one can be successfully against him (Rom. 8:31). That man's children will have a place of refuge under God's wings when evil attacks.

27. Trust in God is a source of spiritual strength and vitality, enabling one to avoid the snares of death.

28. The size, contentment, and loyalty of the populace determine the glory of a king. It is a small honor for a prince to hold the title if he has few or no people over whom to rule.

29. A man who is patient under provocation shows great insight. He who is easily provoked promotes folly and holds it up to public view.

30. A sound heart here means a satisfied mind. Thus Knox says, "Peace of mind is health of body."

Envy and passion are bad for a person's health. Dr. Paul Adolph confirms this when he writes, "Some of the most important causes of so-called nervous diseases which psychiatrists recognize are guilt, resentment (an unforgiving spirit), fear, anxiety, frustration, indecision, doubt, jealousy, selfishness, and boredom. Unfortunately, many psychiatrists, while definitely effective in tracing the causes of emotional disturbances which cause disease, have significantly failed in their methods of dealing with these disturbances because they omit faith in God as their approach."

31. Whoever takes advantage of the poor insults his Creator. George Herbert said that man is God's image, but a poor man is Christ's stamp as well.

The second line means that those who have compassion on the poor honor God in the process.

32. "When the wicked is paid in his own coin, there is an end of him; at death's door, the just still hope" (Knox). Judas is an illustration of the first line, and Paul, of the second.

33. The clause, "Wisdom abides in the mind of a man of understanding" may mean (1) that wisdom is at home there, or (2) that the man doesn't needlessly parade everything he knows.

The second line is more difficult. It may mean (1) you will soon find out what is in the heart of fools (AV); (2) wisdom is not known in the heart of fools (RSV); (3) "wisdom must clamor loudly before being recognized by fools" (Berkeley margin).

34. In order for a nation to be great, its leaders and people must have upright, moral characters. Corruption, graft, bribery, "dirty tricks," scandal, and all forms of civil unrighteousness bring disgrace to a country.

35. A ruler looks with favor on a servant who acts wisely (compare Joseph, Mordecai, Daniel). His anger is directed toward those who act shamefully. "The king favors an able minister; his anger is for the incompetent" (Moffatt).

CHAPTER 15

Much of this chapter is devoted to the subject of speech.

1. A gentle or conciliating reply prevents anger from bursting forth or from increasing. If you answer a man with a harsh word, it stirs up his fleshly nature, and pretty soon you have a violent quarrel on your hands.

"I once lived where my neighbor's garden was divided from me only by a very imperfect hedge. He kept a dog, and his dog was a shockingly bad gardener, and did not improve my plants. So, one evening, while I walked alone, I saw this dog doing mischief and being a long way off, I threw a stick at him, with some earnest advice as to his going home. This dog, instead of going home, picked up my stick, and came to me with it in his mouth, wagging his tail. He dropped the stick at my feet and looked up to me most kindly. What could I do but pat him and call him a good dog, and regret that I had ever spoken roughly to him?" (C. H. Spurgeon).

2. A wise man's tongue pours forth helpful information. He knows what, when, where, and how to speak. Foolishness gushes like a torrent from the mouth of fools.

3. God is omniscient, that is, He knows everything. Nothing is hidden from Him. He is aware of every word, act, thought, and motive, whether good or bad. This caused David to exclaim, "Such knowledge is too wonderful for me; it is too high, I cannot attain to it" (Psa. 139:6 NASB).

4. Wholesome, gracious speech refreshes, soothes, and revives. Perverse, malicious talk can be heartbreaking.

5. We have met this fool before. He considers his father a back number whose ideas are old-fashioned and whose advice is worthless. The wise son heeds parental instruction and benefits by it. He *is prudent,* and he *becomes more prudent.*

6. Those who were reared in a godly home can testify to the truth of the first line. Even though the parents might not have been affluent, they left their children a spiritual heritage of immense value.

The ill-gotten gain of the unscrupulous man brings trouble on himself and his family. Can you find a good illustration of this in the first ten chapters of Joshua?

7. A wise man's conversation is full of helpful information. The foolish man can't edify anyone else because his own mind is empty.

8. The first line teaches the worthlessness of ritual without reality. A wicked man may bring costly offerings to the Lord but God despises them. He wants the man's life to be clean first. "To obey is better than sacrifice" (1 Sam. 15:22). God delights in the humble prayer of a righteous person; "the sacrifices of God are a broken spirit: a broken and a contrite heart, O God, thou wilt not despise" (Psa. 51:17).

9. The way a wicked man lives displeases the Lord greatly. He gets real pleasure out of the person who lives in obedience to His Word.

10. There are two ways of looking at this proverb. It may be describing two different men—the wayward and the unteachable, and the punishment they earn—stern correction and death respectively. Or it may be describing the same man in both lines. At first his waywardness brings him severe discipline. But he refuses to learn from it and so plunges on to death.

11. Hell and destruction mean Sheol and Abaddon, and are symbolic of the unseen world beyond the grave. If God knows all about what transpires in death and in the hereafter, how much more does He know the thoughts and secrets of men on earth? "All things are naked and opened unto the eyes of him with whom we have to do" (Heb. 4:13).

12. A scorner resents being corrected. He will not go to a wise person for advice, but to someone who he thinks will tell him what he wants to hear. Such a policy is self-defeating; it only confirms him in his obstinacy and leaves him in the grave of stagnation.

13. A merry heart is reflected in a smiling face, but a broken heart has deeper effects. It causes despondency and despair.

14. The most knowledgeable people never stop in their pursuit of knowledge. The mouths of fools chew vacantly on folly. "The wise grow wiser, the foolish more dense."

15. This seems to contrast the pessimist and the optimist. The first is always down-in-the-mouth. He is gloomy, fearful, and negative. The optimist always seems to be on top. He enjoys life to the full.

16. A poor believer is better off than a wealthy worrywart. Wealth has troubles attached. The life of faith is the carefree life.

17. A plate of vegetables in an atmosphere of love is better than a filet mignon roast where there is strife. Moffatt says, "Better is a dish of vegetables, than the best beef served with hatred."

A stalled ox is one that has been raised in a stall and given the best feed; its meat is tender and delicious.

Joseph R. Sizoo says, "In a nearby city I visited one of the most luxurious estates I've ever seen in America. Within the house were Italian fireplaces, Belgian tapestries, Oriental rugs, and rare paintings. I said to a friend, 'How happy the people must have been who lived here!' 'But they weren't,' he replied. 'Although they were millionaires, the husband and wife never spoke to each other. This place was a hotbed of hatred! They had no love for God or for one another' " (Our Daily Bread).

18. A hot-tempered man is always spreading strife. A wiser man knows how to avoid contentions or cool them down after they have started.

19. The path of the lazy man is beset with all kinds of difficulties. Maybe he tries to use these as an excuse for doing nothing. The way of the righteous is a smooth, well-paved highway.

20. A clean-living son brings great satisfaction to his dad. But the wayward son treats his mother with contempt by disobeying her will and disregarding her tears.

21. A stupid man enjoys his stupidity. He has never known anything better. The wise man gets his joy out of a life of sobriety and morality.

A pig enjoys wallowing in the mire, whereas a sheep wants the clean pasture.

22. When men act singly, without consulting others, their programs often fail. It is safer to get a broad range of information and advice. Men who have had experience can warn against dangers to be avoided, can suggest the best methods, etc.

23. There is genuine satisfaction in being able to give an honest, helpful answer. Also a timely word—spoken at just the right time to meet a particular need—is splendid. Compare Isaiah 50:4, ". . . a word in season to him who is weary." Jesus knows how to speak that word.

24. The wise man's pathway goes upward toward life, that he may avoid the pathway that leads downward to death and destruction. Once again we are reminded of the two roads and two destinies of the human race.

25. The Lord will destroy the estate of the haughty and highhanded, but He will protect the boundaries of the oppressed widow's little farm.

26. God detests the wicked plans of unscrupulous men, but He is pleased with the words of the pure.

27. This proverb may refer primarily to a judge or other public officer who swells his bank account by accepting bribes. In so doing he perverts judgment and corrupts his conduct. But even worse—he brings trouble unlimited on his household. The man who refuses to have anything to do with bribes (gifts) is the one who enjoys life.

28. A good man thinks before he speaks. He meditates on how he ought to reply. The ungodly man opens his mouth and out comes a torrent of profanity, filth, and vileness.

29. The Lord is far from the wicked in the sense that He does not enjoy fellowship with them, and they are not in touch with Him by prayer. Believers have instant audience with the Sovereign of the universe in the throne room of heaven by prayer. "We know that God does not hear sinners; but if any one is God-fearing, and does His will, He hears him" (John 9:31 NASB).

30. A person's beaming countenance is contagious. It gladdens the heart of everyone he meets. Also, good news makes a man's whole being feel good.

31. The man who heeds counsel that leads to the true way of life takes his place among the wise of the earth. The teaching of the Bible in general and the gospel in particular is life-giving counsel.

32. If a man won't listen to godly counsel, it means that he hates himself because he is plunging over the cataract to ruin. The one who receives instruction promotes his own best interests.

33. Trust in the Lord is the discipline that leads to wisdom. Humility is the way to honor.

Lesson Seven
Proverbs 16, 17

CHAPTER 16

The name Jehovah (LORD) occurs nine times in the first eleven verses of this chapter.

1. Man may plan his thoughts in advance, but God is sovereign and overrules all man's words for the accomplishment of His purposes. "Man proposes but God disposes." Balaam, for instance, wanted to curse the people of Israel, but the words came out as a blessing (Num. 22:38; 23:7-10). Or think of Caiaphas, who spoke beyond his own wisdom (John 11:49-52). Herod and Pilate conspired to do to Jesus what God had already appointed to be done (Acts 4:27,28).

It may also mean that though God's persecuted people often plan in advance what to say at their trial, God gives the proper words at the suited time (Matt. 10:19).

2. A man's ways are his outward acts; he judges himself by them and pronounces himself clean. But God sees the motives and intentions of the heart. "Who can discern his errors? Clear thou me from hidden faults" (Psa. 19:12 RV).

3. The best way to insure that our dreams and goals will be achieved is to dedicate our work to the Lord.

"Occasionally we find ourselves disturbed and depressed, even in trying to do the Lord's work. Could anything be further from what God desires? God cannot work through anxious hearts. Whenever a Christian reaches this state, he should stop at once and ask himself, 'Whose work is it?' If it's God's work, never forget the burden of it is His, too. You are not the important person. Christ is! He is at work through us. What should we do then when things do not go well? Go to Him! Anything less than this is disobedience" (J. Allen Blair).

"Prayer: Give me the eye which sees God in all, and the

hand which can serve Him in all, and the heart which can bless Him for all" (Daily Notes).

4. This verse does not suggest that God has created certain men to be damned. The Bible nowhere teaches the doctrine of reprobation. Men are damned by their own deliberate choice, not by God's decree.

The proverb means that God has an end, object, or purpose for everything. There is a result for every cause, a reward or punishment for every act. He has ordained a day of trouble or evil for the wicked, just as He has prepared heaven for those who love Him. "Everything the Lord has made has its destiny; and the destiny of the wicked man is destruction" (TEV).

5. Human pride is hateful to God. As explained previously, "though hand join in hand" means "assuredly" or "certainly."

6. The doctrine of this verse must be studied in the light of all other Scriptures on the subject. It cannot mean that a man is saved by being merciful and truthful; salvation is by grace through faith in the Lord. Only to the extent that mercy and truth are the signs of saving faith can they be said to purge iniquity.

The second part of the proverb is clear on the face of it. By trusting the Lord, men escape misfortune and calamity.

7. Like so many of the proverbs, this is a general rule, but it does have exceptions. "A righteous life disarms opposition." "Goodness has power to charm and win even enemies to itself" (Barnes).

Stanton treated Lincoln with utter contempt. He called him a "low cunning clown" and "the original gorilla." He said there was no need to go to Africa to capture a gorilla when one was available in Springfield, Illinois. Lincoln never retaliated. Instead he made Stanton his war minister, believing that he was the best qualified for the office.

Years later when Lincoln was killed by an assassin's bullet, Stanton looked down on his rugged face and said tearfully, "There lies the greatest ruler of men the world has ever seen."

8. It is better to have a modest income, which is earned honestly, than to have great financial treasures with injustice or with fraud.

9. As we were reminded in verse 1, man goes to great length to plan his career, but the Lord alone determines whether these plans ever come to pass. Saul of Tarsus planned to persecute the saints in Damascus but ended up being one of the saints. Onesimus planned to leave Philemon forever but God brought him back on better terms than ever.

10. Because a king is a representative of God (Rom. 13:1), his edicts and decisions carry authority and finality. Therefore "his mouth shall not transgress in judgment" (ASV).

11. God maintains a Bureau of Standards. He determines weights and measures. When men deal in accordance with His standards, He approves and blesses them.

12. Actually it is abomination for anyone to commit wickedness, but especially for kings. They represent God in their position, and therefore have greater responsibility. The throne rests on a foundation of well-doing.

It should be added that the verse may mean that it is an abomination to kings for their subjects to commit wickedness. Lawful, orderly government must be sustained by righteousness. Where moral standards are abandoned, anarchy prevails.

13. Good kings don't appreciate those who flatter and speak hypocritically. They want men whose word is trustworthy, who are frank and sincere.

14. A king enraged can quickly sentence offenders to death. A wise man will not provoke the ruler needlessly but will seek to pacify him.

15. When the king is joyful, the happiness of his countenance spreads gladness through the realm. His favor is as refreshing as the clouds that bring the latter rain.

16. Earthly riches are not to be compared to wisdom and knowledge. Riches often disappear overnight but divine wisdom remains throughout eternity.

17. The righteous follow the highway of holiness without turning off on the tangents of sin. The one who keeps straight on this highway saves his life from damage and misfortune.

18. A tall tree attracts lightning. So God abases those who are conceited. Stuck-up people usually suffer some humiliating experience, designed to deflate their ego. It takes only a small pin to prick a large balloon.

It was pride that caused the fall of Lucifer—"aspiring pride and insolence for which God threw him from the face of heaven" (Marlowe).

19. It's better to be humble yourself and to be a companion of humble people, than to share the seeming advantages of the proud.

Would'st thou be chief—then lowly serve;
Would'st thou go up—go down;
But go as low as e'er you will,
The Highest has been lower still.

20. The NASB translation is better here: "He who gives attention to the word shall find good, and blessed is he who trusts in the Lord." So the proverb says, "Read your Bible; heed it; and trust the One who wrote it."

21. A man who is truly wise will be acknowledged for his prudence, discernment, and insight. In addition, the pleasant manner in which he speaks will make others more willing to listen to him and to learn. ". . . Sweetness of speech increases persuasiveness" (NASB).

22. Wisdom serves as a source of life and refreshment to its possessor, whereas folly is like a whiplash to a fool. He is punished by his own folly. "Folly is the chastisement of fools" (Berkeley).

23. The speech of a wise man is an index of what is in his mind. He displays his knowledge by what he says. And there is a certain persuasiveness about his statements. He speaks with authority.

24. Kind, gentle words have the qualities of a honeycomb—sweet to the taste and healthful for the body. "To say nice things when we can is a simple benefit we may bring a person, in mind and thence in body" (Kidner).

Watchman Nee told of a woman whose husband never expressed appreciation for anything she had ever done. She worried constantly that she had failed as a wife and mother. Possibly this is what caused her to develop tuberculosis. When she was dying, her husband said to her, "I don't know what we are going to do. You have done so much and done it well." "Why didn't you say that sooner?" she asked, "I have been blaming myself all along, because you never once said 'Well done.'"

25. This repeats 14:12 for emphasis. It seems logical and reasonable that the way to heaven is by being good and doing good. But the true fact is that the only people who will ever get to heaven are sinners saved by grace.

26. "A worker's appetite works for him, for his hunger urges him on" (NASB). He knows that if he doesn't work, he won't collect his paycheck, and without money he can't go to the supermarket to buy food. So if he is ever tempted to stop working, his appetite urges him on.

This is also true in the spiritual realm. A realization of our deep spiritual need drives us to the Word and to prayer.

27. Verses 27-30 give different portraits of wickedness. First we see the wicked man as one who plots (diggeth up) evil, and whose speech is like a scorching fire, burning and injuring.

28. A froward man is one who distorts the truth. By lying, shading the truth, or withholding the facts, he spreads strife. A talebearer separates close (chief) friends.

29. The man of violence seeks to lead his neighbor astray, encouraging him to be a partner in crime (see Rom. 1:32).

30. Facial expressions can have evil connotations. A wink can hint at the connivance of some wickedness, and compressed lips can express the determination to see it through.

31. The "if" should be omitted. The hoary head stands for long life. It is a crown of glory or beauty because it is looked on here as a reward for a righteous life. So this verse is the opposite of Psalm 55:23, "Bloody and deceitful men shall not live out half their days."

32. A man who can control his temper is a greater hero than a military conqueror. Victory in this area is more difficult than in capturing a city. If you don't believe it, try it!

"Peter the Great, although one of the mightiest of the Czars of Russia, failed here. In a fit of temper he struck his gardener, and a few days afterwards the gardener died. 'Alas,' said Peter, sadly, 'I have conquered other nations, but I have not been able to conquer myself!' " (from Winsome Christianity).

33. In the Old Testament and even up to the time of Pentecost, the casting of lots was a legitimate way of determining the will of God. The whole process seemed very much a matter of chance, but God overruled to reveal His guidance.

Today the complete Word of God gives us a general outline of God's will. When we need specific guidance in matters not covered in the Word, we learn His will through waiting on Him in prayer.

CHAPTER 17

1. A piece of zwieback or dry toast eaten in a relaxed

setting is better than a sumptuous meal in an elegant house where there is bickering and unhappiness.

2. A capable servant often rises higher than a foolish son. Thus Solomon's servant, Jeroboam, gained control over ten of the tribes of Israel, leaving Solomon's son, Rehoboam, with only two.

The servant often shares the inheritance with the sons on an equal basis. In Abram's case it looked for a while as if his servant would be his only heir (Gen. 15:2,3).

3. God can do what no crucible or furnace can do. They can test precious metals but He can test the human heart. In the process of testing, He removes the dross and purifies the life until He sees His own image reflected.

When thru' fiery trials thy pathway shall lie,
My grace, all sufficient, shall be thy supply;
The flame shall not hurt thee; I only design
Thy dross to consume, and thy gold to refine.

4. People with wicked hearts listen eagerly to people with wicked lips. They welcome lies, unfounded rumors, false accusations. Liars, in turn, like to listen to scandal, slander, and malicious talk. In that sense, the kind of talk a man feeds on is a barometer of what he is at heart.

5. We have already seen in 14:31 that whoever mocks the poor insults God (see Jas. 5:1-4). Whoever takes a heartless satisfaction in calamities (which almost invariably make people poor) will be punished by the Lord. The book of Obadiah pronounces doom on Edom for rejoicing when Jerusalem fell.

6. A numerous and godly posterity brings honor to an old man (see Psa. 127:3-5; 128:3). Children likewise can be grateful for godly ancestors. There is no reason for a generation gap here.

7. Noble and excellent speech seems out of place in the mouth of a boorish fool. Even more unsuitable are lying lips in a prince. You expect more from a prince.

The world expects more from those of us who are children of God. They have higher standards for us than they do for themselves.

8. A bribe serves like a good luck charm, or so its owner thinks. Wherever he uses it, it performs wonders for him, opening doors, obtaining favors and privileges, or getting him out of trouble.

9. The man who refuses to remember an offense against him seeks love and friendship. The one who insists on digging up past grievances only succeeds in alienating a friend.

"When we learn to love, we also learn to cover, to forget, and to overlook many faults in others" (Adams).

One woman to another: "Don't you remember the mean thing she said about you?"

The other woman: "I not only don't remember; I distinctly remember forgetting!"

George Washington Carver was refused admission to a college because he was black. Years later, when someone asked him for the name of the college, he answered, "It doesn't matter!" Love had conquered.

10. A simple rebuke makes a deeper impression on a wise man than a severe beating on a fool. Usually people who are sensitive do not need harsh forms of discipline. But those who are unfeeling and indifferent require the sledgehammer treatment. It is hard for them to think that they are ever wrong.

11. "A wicked man seeks only rebellion" (Berkeley). He is unwilling to submit to lawful authority. He is determined to have his own way. The cruel messenger who will be sent against the rebel may be the arresting officer sent by the king, or it may be the messenger of death sent by God.

12. A bear robbed of her cubs is fierce and unmanageable. But she is not nearly as dangerous as a fool in a fit of temper. Once he gets some crazy idea in his head, nothing will stop him.

13. A curse rests upon the house of any man who repays a kindness with an injury. David repaid his loyal general, Uriah, with treachery, and, as a result, brought misery upon his house (2 Sam. 12:9,10).

14. When a hole develops in a dike, the water rushing through it enlarges the hole rapidly. It is the same with quarrels. Minor disputes have a way of growing to major proportions. So it is better to stop while a dispute is still insignificant. Otherwise you may be plunged into a great war soon.

15. God hates miscarriages of justice. To acquit the guilty or to condemn the innocent are equally abhorrent to Him. Our law courts are filled with this today, but men will give an account for it all when they stand before God. The dictum "Justice, justice you shall follow" echoes down through the corridors of history.

16. A person is foolish to go to great expense to get an education if he doesn't really mean business. To be a good learner, one must be highly motivated. He must have "a mind to learn" (Moffatt).

A second and more probable meaning of the proverb is this: a fool should not spend money for wisdom when he doesn't have the ability to grasp things in the first place. "Why is this—a price in the hand of a fool to buy wisdom, when he has no capacity?" (Berkeley). He thinks he can buy wisdom as if it were a loaf of bread. He doesn't realize that he must have an understanding heart.

17. A true friend loves in adversity as well as in prosperity. Often it takes hard times to show which friends are genuinely loyal.

A brother is born for adversity, that is, one of the great privileges of brotherhood is to be at your side when you need him most.

It is not hard to find the Lord Jesus in this verse.

There's not an hour that He is not near us,
No, not one! No, not one!

No night so dark but His love can cheer us,
No, not one! No, not one!

18. This verse modifies the previous one by showing that love should not be without discernment. It would be a case of bad judgment to agree to guarantee a friend's debts in the event that he should default. Any man who needs a surety is a bad credit risk. Why be surety for a bad credit risk?

19. The man who loves sin loves strife, and vice versa. The man who exalts his gate is one who (1) talks arrogantly (Moffatt); (2) loudly proclaims his wealth; or (3) lives luxuriously and perhaps beyond his means. This man courts destruction.

20. A perverse heart never wins, and a deceitful tongue never prospers. They invite mischief and prevent happiness.

21. The father of a senseless dolt lives with sorrow. There is no joy in being the parent of a "dull thud."

22. Here again we learn that a person's mental outlook has a lot to do with recovery from sickness or accident. A cheerful disposition is a powerful aid to healing. A broken, disconsolate heart saps a person's vitality.

In a footnote on this verse, the Berkeley Version comments: "Up-to-date therapy, unsurpassed."

"Today's doctors tell us that a hearty laugh is great exercise. When you emit an explosive guffaw, they say, your diaphragm descends deep into your body and your lungs expand, greatly increasing the amount of oxygen being taken into them. At the same time, as it expands sideways, the diaphragm gives your heart a gentle, rhythmic massage. That noble organ responds by beating faster and harder. Circulation speeds up. Liver, stomach, pancreas, spleen, and gall bladder are all stimulated—your entire system gets an invigorating lift. All of which confirms what that sage old Greek, Aristotle, said about laughter more than 2000 years ago: 'It is a bodily exercise precious to health' " (Paul Brock).

But not all laughter is healthful. Howard Pollis, a psychology professor at the University of Tennessee reports that when laughter and smiling are used in an aggressive way—to sneer at, to ridicule, to embarrass—they are "nonhealthy" and can really do more harm to the laugher than the one who is laughed at.

"A broken spirit drieth the bones." Writer Blake Clark agrees: "Emotions can make you ill. They can make hair fall out by the handful, bring on splitting headaches, clog nasal passages, make eyes and nose water with asthma and allergies, tighten the throat with laryngitis, make skin break out in a rash, even cause teeth to drop out. Emotions can plague one's insides with ulcers and itises, give wives miscarriages, make husbands impotent—and much more. Emotions can kill."

23. A wicked man takes a bribe out of his pocket to influence the decision of the judge in his favor.

24. A man of understanding sets wisdom as the goal before his eyes and goes right toward it. A fool has no definite ambition. Rather than search for wisdom, which requires discipline, he wanders in fantasy all over the world.

25. One of the great sorrows of parenthood is to have a child who causes nothing but grief and bitterness.

26. "It is also not good to fine the righteous, nor to strike the noble for their uprightness" (NASB). Yet this perversion of justice takes place every day.

27. "He who restrains his words has knowledge, and he who has a cool spirit is a man of understanding" (RSV). Rash speech and quick temper betray a shallow character.

28. You can't tell a fool by his facial appearance; he might look ever so wise. "With closed lips he may be counted sensible" (Moffatt).

"At times, it is better to keep your mouth shut and let people wonder if you're a fool than to open it and remove all doubt" (James G. Sinclair).

Lesson Eight
Proverbs 18—20

CHAPTER 18

1. The difficulty of this proverb is seen in the widely different interpretations that are given.

"He who separates himself seeks his own desire, he quarrels against all sound wisdom" (NASB). This is the nonconformist who is going to have his own way even if it conflicts with tested knowledge or approved methods. He flies in the face of sound wisdom by his self-assertion.

The RSV is quite different: "He who is estranged seeks pretexts to break out against all sound judgment." In other words, the man who becomes alienated looks for excuses to justify all kinds of irresponsible conduct.

Knox's translation is somewhat similar and needs no explanation: "None so quick to find pretexts, as he that would break with a friend; he is in fault continually."

Jewish commentators understand the proverb to commend the life of separation from sin and folly. The man who does this desires his own higher interests and mingles himself with all true wisdom. But this interpretation is improbable, though true.

2. A fool refuses to listen to people with understanding; he is interested only in expressing his own opinion (RSV), or in displaying what he is (Moffatt).

3. "Wickedness is followed by shame; dishonor has disgrace in its wake." Which is another way of saying that outward shame and reproach come on the heels of inward wickedness and baseness.

4. Generally speaking, a man's words don't give him away. They are a deep pool, hiding his true thoughts and motives.

By way of contrast, the fountain of wisdom is a gushing

stream (RSV). In other words, wisdom's message is clear and transparent.

Moffatt understands the verses as saying that the words of a wise man are a deep pool, a flowing stream, a fountain of life. They are profound, not shallow; flowing, not brackish; refreshing, not insipid.

5. God here condemns the reversal of moral judgments. To show partiality to the wicked is, in effect, condoning their wickedness. To deprive the righteous of justice is what Lowell called putting Truth on the scaffold and Wrong on the throne.

6. A loud-mouthed fool is always trying to pick a fight or start trouble. A drunkard excels at this, but all he succeeds in doing is bringing black eyes, contusions, and abrasions on himself.

7. A fool's speech is his downfall. His reckless and foul language bring about his eventual ruin.

8. The correct meaning here is that a gossip's words are like delicious tidbits (rather than wounds); they are eagerly devoured by the listeners. It is almost as if the listeners say, "Yum, yum. I like that. Tell me more."

9. The lazy or slack man has much in common with a destroyer; they both cause great havoc or devastation. "Waster" (AV) means one who lays waste, not one who discards things carelessly or needlessly.

"We know today that it is shoddy workmanship in cars, airplanes, buildings, and the like which is the cause of fatal accidents. This is also true in some offices and leadership in the church, where negligence of responsibility may lead to a breakdown of fellowship. A church may be disintegrated through foolish negligence and laziness as well as by Satanic attack" (Griffiths).

10. The name of the Lord stands for the Lord Himself. The Lord is a place of refuge and protection for those who trust in Him. Therefore, in the moment of fierce temptation, call upon the name of the Lord, and He will preserve you from sinning.

11. The rich man trusts his wealth to protect him. In his conceit, he thinks it will serve as a high wall to guard him from danger of every kind. But his riches fail him when he needs them most.

Verse 10 is fact: verse 11 is fiction.

The righteous man of verse 10 trusts in fact, the rich man of verse 11 is fiction.

12. Pride has one foot in the grave and another on a banana skin. Humility walks securely toward honor. "Look not at pride only as an unbecoming temper, nor at humility as a decent virtue—one is all hell and the other all heaven" (Wm. Law).

13. A man should get all the facts before giving his opinion. Otherwise he will be embarrassed when the full details are made known. There are two sides to every question—every divorce, every quarrel, etc. Don't agree with a person if you have not heard the other person's side.

14. A man's spirit can bear up under all kinds of physical infirmities, but a broken heart is far more difficult to endure. "The writer is saying that emotional trouble is far more serious than physical trouble" (Adams).

Dr. Paul Adolph tells of an elderly patient who was recovering satisfactorily in the hospital from a broken hip. When it was time for her to go home, her daughter told her that arrangements had been made for her to go to an old people's home. Within a few hours, the patient showed general physical deterioration and she died in less than a day—"not of a broken hip but of a broken heart."

A man who had faced the horrors of concentration camp with gallantry discovered after his release that it was his own son who had informed on him. "The discovery beat him to his knees and he died. He could bear the attack of an enemy, but the attack of one whom he loved killed him."

15. The wise man never comes to the place where he ceases to learn. His mind is always open to instruction, and his ear is receptive to knowledge.

16. A man's bribe or gratuity buys his way into the presence of those whom he wishes to influence.

It is also true, as the proverb is sometimes used, that a man's spiritual gift provides opportunities for him to exercise it. If he can teach or preach the Word, for instance, he will have plenty of openings. But that is not the meaning of this verse.

17. When a man tells his side of the story, it seems very convincing and you are apt to believe him. But when his adversary comes and asks him a few leading questions, then it may appear that he was not so right after all.

18. When believers in the Old Testament cast lots, they were actually appealing to the Lord to settle matters for which they felt themselves inadequate. The lot provided a just and peaceful settlement of matters between powerful contenders who might otherwise have resorted to force.

We too should let the Lord be the final Judge when difficulties arise with others. We can do this, not by casting lots, but by reading and obeying the Bible, by confessing our faults one to another, by prayer, and by the inward witness of the Spirit.

19. Quarrels between close relatives are often the hardest to mend. It is easier to conquer a fortified city than to effect reconciliation between offended brothers. Their contentions are like the bars of a castle—cold, straight, and immovable. Civil wars are always the bitterest.

20. We sometimes say that a man has to eat his words. If they have been good words, they will yield satisfaction to him. He will be rewarded according to the nature of his speech.

21. The tongue has great potential for good or evil. Those who love to use it a lot must be prepared to take the consequences.

22. The word "good" is implied before "wife." A man who finds a good wife finds a treasure. It is a token of the Lord's favor when he finds a godly, helpful bride.

23. Poor people often speak softly, humbly, pleadingly. Rich people, on the other hand, can be rough and overbearing, but not all rich people have bad manners!

24. Here again we have a proverb with many interpretations.

If we follow the AV, the thought is that friendliness wins friends, and that some friends are closer than others.

The NASB, ASV, and Darby say that a man who has many friends will come to ruin, but that there is a friend who sticks closer than a brother. This means that it is better to have one true friend than a host of friends who will lead you astray.

The RSV reads, "There are friends who pretend to be friends, but there is a friend who sticks closer than a brother." This presents a contrast between fair-weather friends and those who are loyal through thick and thin.

Happily, most versions agree on the second line—that there is a friend who sticks closer than a brother. "All consideration of this great verse leads us at last to one place, to One Person. He is the Friend of sinners. There comment ceases. Let the heart wonder and worship (G. Campbell Morgan).

CHAPTER 19

1. The contrast is between a poor man who is honest and a devious (and perhaps rich) fool who distorts the truth. The poor man has it all over the fool; he is better off.

2. The ASV margin reads, "Also, desire without knowledge is not good." This man knows what he wants to do, but he doesn't know how to do it, so he goes off "half-cocked."

Haste only adds to his misery. He is in too much of a hurry to ask for directions or to follow them if given, so he misses the way and goes around in circles.

3. When men make a mess of their lives, they turn around and blame the Lord. Thus, Adam tried to put the blame on God with the words "the woman whom thou gavest to be with me . . ." (Gen. 3:12).

More than we know, apostasy has its seeds in moral failure. A man engages in some form of immorality, then instead of confessing and forsaking the sin, he turns away from the Christian faith and rages against God. W. F. Adeney comments, "It is monstrous to charge the providence of God with the consequences of actions that He has forbidden."

4. The fact that wealth makes many friends is a proof of the innate selfishness of the human heart. The poor man is deserted by his neighbor because the latter wants only those friendships that will benefit him.

5. Those who give false testimony or engage in other forms of dishonesty will surely be punished by the Lord, if they are never caught in this life.

6. The prince here is a generous or powerful man. Many try to cultivate his friendship with the hope of getting favors. Men befriend those from whom they hope to benefit.

7. The relatives of a poor man often desert him. Much more do his friends give him the cold shoulder. He appeals to them pathetically for help and sympathy, but they have vanished.

8. It is a form of enlightened self-interest to seek wisdom and common sense. And to hold on to understanding and insight is a sure road to success.

9. We should not be surprised at the frequency with which this is repeated. After all, one of the Ten Commandments deals with perjury (Exod. 20:16).

10. Luxury (delight) is not fitting for a fool. He doesn't know how to act in the midst of culture and refinement. Neither does a slave know how to act in a position of authority. He treats his former superiors arrogantly.

11. A man of good sense knows how to control his temper. He can graciously overlook it when somebody wrongs him. The big-heartedness which David frequently displayed toward Saul illustrates the proverb well.

12. The king's anger, like a lion's roaring, warns offenders of danger ahead. His favor to those who are obedient subjects is as gentle and refreshing as dew.

Romans 13:1-7 sets forth these two aspects of governmental authority and cautions, "Wherefore ye must needs be subject, not only for wrath, but also for conscience sake" (v. 5).

13. Two things that make domestic life miserable are a wayward son and a nagging wife. The former brings grief to his father, and the latter is as annoying as a persistent drip of water on metal.

14. You can inherit real estate and money from parents, but only the Lord can provide a prudent wife. She is a special gift of God.

This reminds us of Isaac and Rebecca's storybook marriage, of which it is said, "The thing proceedeth from the Lord" (Gen. 24:50). It was a marriage that was arranged in heaven.

15. Laziness is like a drug that casts a man into a deep sleep. Idle people court poverty and hunger.

This is true in connection with Bible study and prayer.

16. The one who obeys the commandments of the Lord is doing what is best for himself in the long run, both physically and spiritually. The man who lives recklessly and carelessly will perish.

17. Giving to the poor is lending to the Lord. God will not only return the amount loaned but will pay good interest as well. Even a cup of cold water given in His name will be rewarded (Matt. 10:42).

"A father once gave his boy a half dollar, telling him he could do with it as he pleased. Later when he asked about it, the little fellow said he had lent it to someone. 'Did you get good security?' inquired his father. 'Yes, I gave it to a poor beggar who looked hungry!' 'O how foolish you are. You'll never get it back!' 'But Dad, *I have the best security;* for the Bible says, he that giveth to the poor *lendeth to the Lord!*' Thinking this over, the Christian father was so pleased that he gave his son another half dollar! 'See!' said the boy. '*I told you I'd get it again,* only I didn't think it would come so soon!' " (Henry Bosch).

> We lose what on ourselves we spend,
> We have, as treasures without end,
> Whatever, Lord, to Thee we lend,
> Who givest all.
>
> C. Wordsworth

18. Discipline your son while he is still young and teachable. Corporal punishment, administered fairly and in an atmosphere of genuine love, will not harm him but, on the contrary, will do him an enormous amount of good.

The second line should read "do not set your heart on his destruction" (RSV). This means you should not let his life be ruined by your refusal to punish him. Permissiveness is cruelty. It could also mean, of course, "Don't become so angry that you are in danger of overpunishing him."

19. A hot-headed man will suffer for it. Even if you deliver him from the consequences of his vile temper, he will soon be at it again, and you will have to deliver him again.

20. Listen to sound advice and receive instruction in early life, so you'll be intelligent in later life. As someone has said, "Wisdom is a long-term investment."

21. Man makes all kinds of plans, but it is the purposes of

God that come to pass. "Man has his wickedness but God has His way." Ultimately man can do nothing against the truth (2 Cor. 13:8).

22. Darby's translation of this verse is priceless: "The charm of a man is his kindness; and a poor man is better than a liar." The quality that endears a man to you is kindness. That's what makes him to be desired as a friend.

A poor man who has nothing but sympathy to offer is better than a rich man who promises help but doesn't deliver it.

23. Trust in the Lord is the pathway to life. The one who rests in Jehovah has every reason to be satisfied. He will not be overtaken with calamity.

24. "The sluggard buries his hand in the dish, and will not even bring it back to his mouth" (Berkeley). He reaches into the bowl of potato chips but is too lazy to lift them to his mouth. They are too heavy.

25. Even if you smite a scorner, he won't change, but at least some impressionable onlookers might learn a lesson. This is reminiscent of 1 Timothy 5:20, "Them that sin rebuke before all, that others also may fear."

You don't have to strike a man of understanding. A word of reproof will make him correct his error and grow wiser in the process.

26. A son who assaults (NASB) or slanders (Berkeley) his father and evicts his mother from the home is shameful and disgraceful himself (NASB) and brings disgrace and reproach to his heartbroken parents (ASV). It is small thanks for all his parents have done for him.

27. This proverb is like a diamond; every way you turn it, it sparkles with new light. The three most probable interpretations are these.

The Authorized Version says, "Cease, my son, to hear the instruction that causeth to err from the words of knowledge." Excellent advice for young people in schools and colleges where the Bible is under attack! Better to sacrifice a college career than to subject yourself to a barrage of doubts and denials.

The RSV and Berkeley are probably more accurate: "Cease, my son, to hear instruction only to stray from the words of knowledge." There is no sense in getting good instruction if you are not going to obey it. You are wasting your own time and the teacher's, and increasing your load of guilt. "It is better not to know, than, knowing, to fail to do."

The third interpretation is a warning: "Stop listening to instruction, my son, and you will stray from the words of knowledge" (NIV).

28. A worthless witness cares nothing about justice (except when he is on trial). He greedily swallows (ASV) or spreads (NASB) iniquity. He resembles Eliphaz's description of man, drinking iniquity like water (Job 15:16).

29. While scorners and fools play to the balconies from the stage of human history, punishment and judgment are waiting in the wings. As soon as the curtain is drawn, the inevitable meeting will take place.

CHAPTER 20

1. Wine does mock men but here the thought is that it causes men to become mockers or scorners. Strong drink converts them into brawlers.

Wine is made from grapes, strong drink from grain.

They both lead men astray. First a man becomes a social drinker, then a heavy drinker, then an alcoholic. He tries to shake off the habit, but he is held as if by chains. Christ gives power to break the chains, but first man must want deliverance.

2. When a king is angry, fear spreads throughout his court. That fear is like the lion's roar, warning of danger. Whoever provokes the king takes his life in his hands.

The lesson for us is found in Romans 13:4: "He (i.e., the ruler) is the minister of God to thee for good. But if thou do that which is evil, be afraid; for he beareth not the sword in vain: for he is the minister of God, a revenger to execute wrath upon him that doeth evil."

3. An honorable man makes a point of keeping aloof from strife. A fool isn't happy unless he's quarreling with someone.

4. "Plowing time in Palestine is in November and December, when the wind blows commonly from the North" (Barnes). The sluggard uses the cold weather to excuse his inaction. Without the plowing there can be no planting, and without the planting no harvest. He'll go out looking for grain in his fields and wonder why it isn't there.

5. A man's thoughts and intentions are often hidden deeply in his mind. He will not generally bring them to the surface. But a person of discernment knows how to draw them out by wise questions. For example, a good counselor can help a person bring crooked thinking to the light and thus remedy it.

6. It is not difficult to find those who profess to be loyal, but it is another thing to find those who are faithful. There is a difference between what men are, and what they want others to think they are. It is the difference between "person" and "personality."

7. A godly man walks in honesty and holiness. His children come into a noble heritage and benefit from his life and example.

8. "A king who sits on the throne of judgment winnows all evil with his eyes" (Berkeley). When Christ sits upon His throne of judgment, His all-seeing eyes, like flames of fire, will see through pretense and sift all evidence.

9. By his own efforts, no one can cleanse himself from sin. If a man thinks he is pure, he is a victim of pure delusion.

But there is cleansing through the precious blood of Christ. True believers have "washed their robes, and made them white in the blood of the Lamb" (Rev. 7:14).

> The blood that purchased our release, and purged our crimson stains,
> We challenge earth and hell to show a sin it cannot cleanse.

10. God hates deceitful weights and measurements. This includes any dishonest device to benefit self at the expense of others. It includes the butcher's trick of resting his finger on the scales when he is weighing the meat. And it even includes the practice of demanding stricter standards from others than we do from ourselves.

11. The basic nature of a person reveals itself early in life. Some children are downright ornery, others are pleasant. "The child is father of the man." He carries his character into adulthood, whether for good or for evil.

12. God made the ear and the eye. What can this mean but that they belong to Him and should be used for His glory?

13. Don't overindulge in sleep, lest you land in the poorhouse. Get up and go to work. You'll earn money to pay your rent, buy your groceries, and give to the work of the Lord.

14. This is an old buyer's trick. As he looks over the used car, he squawks about its dents, its worn tires, its noisy engine, and its hideous color. The seller hadn't realized it was such a junkheap; he naively lowers the price. The buyer gives him the money, then goes and boasts to his friends about his tremendous bargain.

15. A person may wear gold jewelry and precious gems, but the best adornment is wise speech. Wear this!

16. "Take a man's garment when he has given surety for a stranger, and hold him in pledge when he gives surety for foreigners" (RSV). Any man who is foolish enough to make financial guarantees for people he doesn't know is a bad credit risk. If you have any dealings with him, be sure that he puts up plenty of collateral so that you will be protected in case he reneges or goes bankrupt.

17. Any form of wealth gained dishonestly might yield momentary satisfaction, but eventually it will prove as unpleasant and aggravating as a mouthful of gravel. This condemns falsifying tax returns, fudging on expense accounts, bribing inspectors, labeling dishonestly, and advertising product differences that don't exist.

18. A pooling of advice is desirable before making any plans. No general makes war without consulting with other military experts.

19. A gossip betrays confidences. Therefore, don't associate with a blabber, because if he talks against others to you, you can be sure that he will talk against you to others.

20. Under the law of Moses, cursing one's parents was a capital offense (Exod. 21:17). This should give pause to young people today who are hostile toward their parents. Unless this bitterness is resolved, it will lead to temporal obscurity and eternal perdition.

21. The prodigal son obtained his share of the inheritance hastily, but he lost it just as quickly. But this proverb is true also of any get-rich-quick schemes. Easy come, easy go.

22. Don't seek vengeance on your enemies. Vengeance is the Lord's. He will repay. Commit your way to the Lord. He will deliver you and vindicate you.

23. Adam Clarke worked for a silk merchant who suggested to him that he should stretch the silk when measuring it for a customer. Adam's reply was, "Your silk may stretch, sir, but my conscience won't." God honored Adam Clarke by enabling him years later to write a commentary on the Bible.

24. This verse emphasizes God's sovereignty and not man's free will, though both are true. The thought is that God is sovereign over human affairs and He knows what is best for us. Therefore, we ought to look to Him for direction, and not try to be the masters of our fate.

25. " 'Tis perilous to say rashly, 'This is sacred!' and then reconsider your vow" (Moffatt). It is dangerous to dedicate something to the Lord, and then to have second thoughts about it. Before making a vow, a man should be sure that he is able to fulfill it and that he definitely intends to.

26. A wise king does not tolerate wicked men. He brings the threshing wheel over them, that is, he separates them from the righteous, brings them to trial and punishes them.

27. The spirit of man in this verse is generally taken to refer to the conscience. It is given to us by the Lord and serves as a lamp, throwing light on our thoughts, motives, affections, and actions. It approves and reproves the innermost thoughts and intents of our lives (see Rom. 2:14,15).

28. A leader who is loving and true will have the respect and support of his subjects. He maintains his position of authority by love, not by tyranny.

29. One of the prominent characteristics of young men is their strength, while the gray hair of old men is associated with wisdom and experience. Every church needs both—strength for service and age for wise counsel.

30. "Blows that wound cleanse away evil, and are strokes that reach the innermost parts" (Berkeley).

The thought seems to be that physical punishment has value in dealing with moral evil. A child remembers the pain of the last spanking when he is tempted to steal from his mother's purse.

Lesson Nine
Proverbs 21—23

CHAPTER 21

1. Just as a channel or canal directs the flow of water, so the Lord rules and overrules a king's thoughts and actions. This is an encouragement to Christians under oppressive governments or to missionaries taking the gospel to hostile lands.

2. A man is not a valid judge of his own life or service; he judges by outward appearances. The Lord judges the thoughts and motives of the heart.

3. The Lord is not as pleased with burnt offerings and sacrifices as with obedience to His voice (1 Sam. 15:22). God is not a ritualist. What He wants is inward reality.

4. This proverb lists three things that are sin in God's sight: haughty eyes, i.e., the outward expression of conceit; a proud heart, i.e., the inward reservoir; and the lamp of the wicked (RSV), which may mean their prosperity, happiness, life, or hope.

5. This verse contrasts those who work diligently for their living with those who seek to get rich overnight. The first are assured of plenty; the second, of poverty.

6. Those who seek riches through fraud and falsehood are chasing the wind. They are pursuing that which will elude them, and they will perish in the process. Their position is like that of a desert traveler chasing a mirage; it proves to be a snare of death for him.

7. "The violence of the wicked will drag them away, because they refuse to act with justice" (NASB). There is a moral principle at work in the universe which guarantees that violence, wickedness, and injustice will never escape unpunished. Never!

8. "Very crooked is the way of a guilty man, but as for the pure, his work is upright" (JND). Guilt causes a man to lie, to hide, to masquerade, to fear, and to act deceitfully. The man who has confessed and forsaken his sins has nothing to hide; he can walk in the light.

9. The houses in Bible lands had flat roofs. This proverb says that it would be better to live alone in the cramped corner of one of those roofs, exposed to heat, cold, rain, snow, wind, and hail, than to live in a house shared by a nagging, cantankerous woman. The storms from without would be more endurable than the tempest inside.

10. A wicked man is always plotting some new crime, and he shows no mercy to his neighbor in perpetrating it. Thus his sin is both deliberate and ruthless. Modern sociological excuses for crime simply don't stand.

11. Even if a scorner might not learn a lesson from the punishment he receives, the naive man will see it and be warned. A wise man doesn't need to be punished; he will learn from simple instruction.

12. The NASB comes to our help here: "The righteous one considers the house of the wicked, turning the wicked to ruin." God is the Righteous One who keeps close watch on all the affairs of ungodly men; at the proper time He throws the switch which brings their doom upon them.

13. The rich man of Luke 16:19-31 was quite unconcerned about the desperate need of the beggar at his gate. In the afterlife, he himself cried for relief but his cry went unanswered.

14. The Bible often reports facts without approving them. Thus it observes that an angry man will quiet down if the offender slips him a gift, and a man who is in a rage is appeased by a bribe tucked in his pocket.

15. "The execution of justice is joy for the righteous, but is terror to the workers of iniquity" (NASB). This is illustrated by the second advent of Christ. It will be a time of ecstasy for the redeemed, but a time of horror for all others (2 Thess. 1:6-9).

16. You meet all kinds of people in Proverbs. This man wanders like a vagrant in the Sahara of sin. When you last see him, he is resting in the assembly of the dead.

17. Instead of giving the satisfaction and fulfilment they promise, pleasure and luxurious living (wine and oil) only serve to impoverish a man. They drain his financial resources and also reduce him to spiritual poverty.

18. In Isaiah 43:3, God says that He gave Egypt as a ransom for His people, Israel. The Lord rewarded Cyrus for liberating the Jews by permitting him to possess Egypt and the neighboring kingdoms.

In a broad sense the verse means that the wicked are punished so that the upright can go free.

19. A touch of sanctified humor! The writer would prefer the discomfort, distance, and loneliness of a desert to being cooped up with a nagging, quarrelsome woman.

20. The contrast here is between the cottage of a wise man where there is a plentiful supply of all good things, and the home of a foolish man where sin, waste, and extravagance lead to scarcity.

We are reminded of the alcoholic who used to sell his furniture and other household goods in order to buy whiskey. After his conversion to Christ, someone said to him, "Surely you don't believe that stuff about Jesus' turning water into wine!" His answer was, "I don't know about turning water into wine, but I know that in my house He turned whiskey into furniture."

21. The point here seems to be that the one who pursues righteousness and steadfast love gets more than he bargained for; in addition he receives life and honor.

22. The Christian casts down strongholds, not with artillery and bombs, but with faith, prayer, and the Word of God (see 2 Cor. 10:4). In the spiritual conflict, wisdom can accomplish what armed might is unable to do.

23. The man who can control his tongue saves himself from stacks of trouble. "Behold, how great a forest is set aflame by such a small fire! And the tongue is a fire, the very world of iniquity; the tongue is set among our members as that which defiles the entire body, and sets on fire the course of our life, and is set on fire by hell" (Jas. 3:5,6 NASB).

24. If you meet a man who is proud, haughty, and arrogant, just call him "Scoffer." That's his name! The name, of course, stands for what a person is. "As his name is, so is he" (1 Sam. 25:25).

25,26. The sluggard is torn apart between his craving for riches on the one hand, and his determination not to exert himself on the other. It's a killing impasse! While he spends his time in a dreamworld of unfulfilled hopes, the righteous man works hard and earns money so that he can give unsparingly to worthy causes.

27. God is "turned off" by the donations of unrepentant sinners, but He hates it even more when a gift is intended to "buy Him off" or induce Him to condone, approve, or bless some wicked scheme.

28. "A false witness will perish, but the word of a man who hears will endure" (RSV). The false witness swears before God that he will tell the truth, then deliberately perjures himself. The man who listens carefully and answers honestly gives testimony that can never be shaken.

29. The brazen face of a wicked man shows that he is confirmed in his iniquity. He has a forehead of brass. The upright man, by being teachable, is safe and certain in his behavior.

30. Man is powerless to outwit God in wisdom, understanding, or strategy. None of his plots can avail against the

Most High. "Every purpose of the Lord shall be performed" (Jer. 51:29).

31. Men may go to elaborate plans to insure military victory, but success in battle comes from the Lord alone. It is better to trust in Him than in horses (or in nuclear weapons) (see Psa. 20:7).

Plumptre reads verses 29 and 30 as follows:
Verse 29: Nothing avails against God.
Verse 30: Nothing avails without God.

CHAPTER 22

1. A good name means a good reputation. It is the fruit of a good character. It is better than great riches because it is more precious, more powerful, and more enduring.

For the same reasons, loving favor is better than silver and gold.

2. Social distinctions are artificial in the sense that we are all of the same human family, and all come from the same Creator. Class distinctions that survive in life are abolished in death.

3. A wise man looks ahead and hides himself from coming judgment. The Israelites did this on the Passover night by sprinkling the blood on their door. We do it by finding refuge in Christ.

The thoughtless pass on in their folly and "pay for it" (Moffatt).

4. Humility and trust in the Lord may seem very dull and commonplace, but don't knock them till you've tried them. They are rewarded with spiritual riches, divine honor, and abundant life.

5. All kinds of difficulties and troubles lie in the way of the perverse man. The man who keeps himself clean avoids them.

6. The usual interpretation of this proverb is that if you train a child properly, he will go on well in later life. Of course there are exceptions, but it stands as a general rule. "It is not hard to make a child or a tree grow right if you train them when they're young, but to make them straighten out after you've allowed things to go wrong is not an easy matter" (Henry Ward Beecher).

Susannah Wesley, the mother of Charles, John, and 15 other children, followed these rules in training them: (1) Subdue self-will in a child and thus work together with God to save his soul. (2) Teach him to pray as soon as he can speak. (3) Give him nothing he cries for and only what is good for him if he asks for it politely. (4) To prevent lying, punish no fault which is freely confessed, but never allow a rebellious, sinful act to go unnoticed. (5) Commend and reward good behavior. (6) Strictly observe all promises you have made to your child.

The proverb can also be understood as encouraging parents to train their children along the lines of their natural talents, rather than forcing them into professions or trades for which they have no native inclination. Thus Kidner says that the verse teaches respect for the child's individuality and vocation, though not for his self-will.

And the proverb may be a warning that if you train a child in the way that he himself wants to go, he will continue to be spoiled and self-centered in later life. "The verse stands not as a promise but as a warning to parents that if they allow a child to train himself after his own wishes (permissively), they should not expect him to want to change these patterns when he matures. Children are born sinners and, when allowed to follow their own wishes, will naturally develop sinful habit responses. The basic thought is that such habit patterns become deep-seated when they have been ingrained in the child from the earliest days" (Adams).

7. Money is power, and it can be used for good or for evil. Too often the rich use it for evil, and perhaps that is why it is called the mammon of unrighteousness.

The borrower is a slave to the lender. Debt is a form of bondage. It requires the payment of exorbitant interest rates. It keeps a man's nose to the grindstone. It limits his mobility and his ability to take advantage of opportunities.

8. The man who sows iniquity gains nothing substantial or worthwhile. His attempt to beat others into submission by anger will be thwarted.

9. The generous man is blessed in showing benevolence to others. By sharing his substance with the poor, he gains present happiness and future reward.

10. When a scorner fails to respond to instruction, correction, and admonition, the next step is eviction. Cast him out! When Ishmael was put out of the house, strife, quarreling, and abuse ceased (Gen. 21:9,10).

11. The man who loves integrity and whose speech is gracious will enjoy royal friendships. God may be the King referred to here.

A little word in kindness spoken,
A motion, or a tear
Has often healed the heart that's broken,
And made a friend sincere.

12. The Lord preserves and perpetuates the knowledge of the truth so that it will never perish from the earth in spite of the rage of demons and men. The same Lord overthrows false teaching and exposes lies.

13. If a sluggard can't find an excuse for not going to work, he will make one up, no matter how ridiculous it is. Here he says that there is a lion in the streets of the city. What would a lion be doing in the city? It's probably nothing more than a cat!

14. The seductive words of a harlot conceal a trap that is difficult to escape from. A man who has estranged himself from God is liable to fall into that trap. This reminds us that

God often abandons men to sin when those men reject the knowledge of God (see Rom. 1:24,26,28).

15. Mischief and self-will are native to the heart of a child, but by applying the board of education to the seat of learning you can rid him of these vices.

"Children need to be corrected and kept under discipline by their parents; and we all need to be corrected by our Heavenly Father (Heb. 12:6,7), and under the correction we must kiss the rod" (Matthew Henry).

16. The employer who gets rich by paying starvation wages will himself suffer want. This will also happen to the man who gives to the rich, presumably in order to court their favor. We should give to those who can't repay us.

17. Verses 17-21 form a paragraph that introduces the proverbs from 22:22 to 24:22. It invites the reader to incline his ear to hear the words of wise men. Perhaps Solomon collected some of these proverbs from others, but the second half of the verse indicates that some of them are his own. The section is entitled "Sayings of the Wise" (NIV).

18. A person should preserve these proverbs in his mind (to remember and obey) and keep them on his lips (to pass them on to others).

19. The reason Solomon made known the proverbs was that the readers might truly trust in the Lord.

20. In the RSV this verse reads, "Have I not written for you thirty sayings of admonition and knowledge?" Some scholars point out that the proverbs that follow (up to 24:22) can be divided into about 30 groupings, as follows:

22:22,23	23:4,5	23:15,16	24:1,2	24:11,12
24,25	6-8	17,18	3,4	13,14
26,27	9	19-21	5,6	15,16
28	10,11	22-25	7	17,18
29	12	26-28	8,9	19,20
23:1-3	13,14	29-35	10	21,22

The Berkeley Bible reads, "Have not I written for you previously of counsels and knowledge. . . ?" The word "previously" is in contrast to "this day" in verse 19.

Still another reading is, "Have I not written to you excellent things of counsels and knowledge?" (NASB, also AV and ASV).

21. The writer aimed at imparting truth so that his pupils might be able to teach others who sent to him for counsel (AV) or so that they might be able to satisfy those (their parents?) who sent them for training.

22,23. This begins the section that ends at 24:22.

No one should take advantage of the defenseless poor. Neither should anyone show injustice to the afflicted at the gate, that is, at the place of judgment. For God pleads the cause of the poor, and He will punish the rich oppressor and the unjust judge.

24,25. Association with an angry, hot-tempered man is bad business. It often makes a man become like the company he keeps. This can really be a snare because in a moment of passion, a man can ruin his life and testimony.

26,27. To strike hands here means to guarantee someone else's debt. It is foolish to do it. If you can't afford to make full payment of the debt, why run the risk of having the furniture taken out of your house, and thus expose yourself to discomfort and shame?

28. The ancient landmarks were stones which indicated the boundaries of a person's property. Dishonest people often moved them during the night to increase the size of their farm at their neighbor's expense.

Spiritually, the ancient landmarks would be the faith once for all delivered unto the saints. The fundamental doctrines of Christianity should not be tampered with.

29. A man who is skillful in his work will be promoted to a position of honor. He will not serve obscure men. This is another reminder that cream rises to the surface. We see it in the lives of Joseph, Moses, Daniel, and Nehemiah.

> The heights by great men reached and kept
> Were not attained by sudden flight,
> But that while their companions slept
> Were toiling upward through the night.

CHAPTER 23

1-3. Here we are warned against gluttony and surfeiting. When we eat with an influential person, we should consider what (AV) or who (JND) is before us. Then we should put the knife to our throat, that is, exercise restraint in eating and drinking.

Verse 3 suggests that someone might be wining and dining us in order to influence us in some way. It isn't a case of unselfish hospitality but a means of using us for some subtle purpose.

4,5. The ceaseless struggle to become rich is a form of "wisdom" to be avoided. It means that you are spending your life pursuing false values and putting your trust in that which doesn't last. Riches have a way of sprouting wings and flying away like an eagle.

6-8. Another social situation to avoid! Don't be a guest of a man who has an evil eye, that is, who grudges you every bite of the food you eat. It's what he thinks, not what he says, that counts. For while he is saying, "Help yourself . . . Have some more," he is actually counting every spoonful you take. The food you eat will go sour in your stomach, and your pleasant words of appreciation will die on your lips.

The Living Bible paraphrases these verses as follows: "Don't associate with evil men; don't long for their favors and gifts. Their kindness is a trick; they want to use you as their pawn. The delicious food they serve will turn sour in your stomach and you will vomit it, and have to take back your words of appreciation for their 'kindness.' "

9. Don't try to teach a dull, stupid person. You are wasting your time on him. He will despise your words of wisdom.

10,11. Don't dishonestly take the property of someone else by secretly moving the boundary stones. Don't take advantage of the defenseless by seizing their fields. For their Avenger (Redeemer) is mighty. You will have to deal with Him. He will plead their cause against you.

12. There is no easy way to gain knowledge. It requires discipline and application. Disregard the ads that promise it in "three easy lessons."

13,14. It is not a kindness to a child to allow him to run wild. The Bible does not condone permissiveness but rather encourages correction with the rod, and promises that the child will not die. This may mean that the beating will not kill him, or that the beating will actually save him from premature and reckless death. It will deliver his soul from Sheol.

Instead of disciplining his wicked sons, Eli rebuked them with a mild "Tut, tut" (1 Sam. 2:22-25). He fostered a permissiveness that brought ruin on his house, on the priesthood, and on the nation.

David too failed in the area of parental discipline. He never displeased Adonijah by correcting him (1 Kgs. 1:6). After making two treasonable attempts to seize the throne, Adonijah was slain by Solomon.

15,16. A father rejoices when his son has a heart that is wise and lips that speak the truth. The teacher experiences this same joy when his pupil receives wisdom and shares it with others. In a similar vein Paul said, "For now we live, if ye stand fast in the Lord" (1 Thess. 3:8). And John said, "I have no greater joy than to hear that my children walk in truth" (3 John 4).

17,18. There is something better than envying the prosperity of the wicked; that is to live in constant fellowship with the Lord. Occupation with the wicked brings discouragement; occupation with the Lord brings delight. So the lesson is to make communion with God the aim of our life. Also, to remember that there is a future day of reckoning for the wicked and a bright hope of reward for the righteous which shall never be disappointed. The "end" (v. 18) looks past death and resurrection to a glorious future in heaven.

19. Whatever others may do, an obedient son should heed instruction, act wisely, and guide his heart in the right way, that is the way of God.

20,21. There are two kinds of drunkards—those who drink too much and those who eat too much. They both make bad company for anyone who wants the good life.

Intemperance takes its toll. The drunkard and the glutton are headed for poverty. The stupor which results from surfeiting will clothe a man in rags.

22. Young people should welcome their father's advice, and not treat their mother with contempt. Old folks have years of experience behind them. Young people should recognize this and try to benefit as much as possible from their experience.

23. We should be willing to pay a great price for truth, but unwilling to surrender it for any consideration. The same goes for wisdom, instruction, and understanding. We should spare no pains to acquire them, but never surrender them for anything in this world.

24,25. Modern custom says, "Give father a tie on Father's Day, and give mother a box of chocolates on Mother's Day." But more rewarding to parents is a son who lives wisely and prudently. Therefore, the exhortation of verse 25: "Let your father and your mother be glad, and let her rejoice who gave birth to you" (NASB).

26-28. The earnest plea, "My son, give me thine heart . . ." introduces solemn warnings against immorality and drunkenness. The writer is saying, "Listen to me carefully and observe the counsel I give you." A prostitute is like a deep, concealed pit, forming a trap for the careless. She is a narrow well—easy to fall into but hard to get out of.

She lies in wait like a robber. She may have a pathological hatred for men, and wreaks her revenge on them by "hooking" them, hence, her slang name "hooker." Daily she adds to the list of unfaithful men whose lives, marriages, and families are torn apart.

29-35. The rest of the chapter is a classic description of a drunkard. He brings all kinds of woe upon himself and staggers from one sorrow to another. His life is marked by contentions, since he is forever trying to pick a fight. He grumbles and complains incessantly, but it never dawns on him that he is the cause of all his troubles. He has bruises, wounds, a black eye—all from fights that were unnecessary and causeless. His eyes are bleery and bloodshot. He sits in the tavern all night, consuming one mixed drink after another.

He is warned against being fascinated by the clear red wine, by its brilliant sparkle, by the way it goes down so smoothly (see RSV). But he doesn't listen, and so he suffers the consequences, which are like the bite of a serpent and the sting of a viper—poisonous and painful.

His eyes see strange things (NASB), a possible reference to the horrors of delirium tremens, the violent mental disturbances caused by excessive and prolonged use of liquor. His conversation is thick, garbled, and vile.

He reels to and fro unsteadily, as if he were bobbing back and forth in the sea, or perched on top of a mast as it rocks crazily from one side to the other.

Someone has clobbered him, but when he regains consciousness, he says that he was not hurt. They mauled him but he did not feel it. As soon as he is completely awake, he plans to go back to the bar for another drink.

Lesson Ten
Proverbs 24—26

CHAPTER 24

1,2. It is not wise to envy the success of wicked men or to desire their company. They have a way of dragging others down to their own levels. And what is that level? Their minds are always planning violence and their conversation centers on troublemaking.

3,4. The house here may refer to a man's life. A great life is not built by wickedness but by godly wisdom. Wickedness wrecks a life but understanding gives it solidity. Wickedness leaves it empty; true knowledge fits it out with precious and pleasant furnishings.

5,6. A wise man can wield greater power than a strong man, and a man of brains is mightier than a man of brawn. War can be waged through wise counselors, and the more wise counselors there are, the better.

7. Wisdom seems to be forever beyond the grasp of a fool. He can never speak with authority, like the elders at the gate of the city do.

8,9. The one who uses his God-given faculties to invent new forms of evil earns the title of "master scoundrel." "The devising of folly is sin" (NASB), and the arrogant scoffer who is brazen in his wickedness earns the contempt of others.

10. One test of a man's worth is how he behaves under pressure. If he gives up when the going is rough, he doesn't have what it takes.

> Christ, if ever my footsteps should falter,
> And I be prepared for retreat;
> If desert and thorn cause lamenting,
> Lord, show me Thy feet.

Thy bleeding feet, Thy nail-scarred feet,
My Jesus, show me Thy feet.

O God, dare I show Thee
My hands and my feet?

—Amy Carmichael

11,12. When innocent people are being led off to gas chambers, ovens, and other modes of execution, it is inexcusable to stand by and not seek to rescue them. It is also useless to plead ignorance. As Dante said, "The hottest places in hell are reserved for those who in a time of great moral crisis maintain their neutrality."

Does this have a voice for those of us who are believers and who are entrusted with the good news of salvation? Men and women are dying without Christ. Jesus said, "Lift up your eyes, and look on the fields: for they are white already to harvest" (John 4:35). Dare we remain neutral?

See the shadows lengthen round us, soon the day-dawn will begin;
Can you leave them lost and lonely? Christ is coming—
Call them in!

13,14. Honey is used here as a symbol of wisdom. Both are beneficial and sweet to the taste.

"Know that wisdom is thus for your soul; if you find it, then there will be a future, and your hope will not be cut off" (NASB). In other words, the man who finds wisdom is assured of a bright future and the realization of all his hopes.

15,16. The unscrupulous man is warned against trying to dispossess a righteous man of his home. Maybe the latter has been overtaken by temporary hardship, and the wicked man is ready to pounce upon his property.

A righteous man may fall into trouble or calamity seven times, but he will recover each time. The wicked can stumble to his ruin in a single misfortune.

17,18. A man of good character should never rejoice when trouble catches up with his adversary, or be happy to see him stumble. If the Lord sees anyone harboring a gloating, vindictive spirit, He will consider that spirit more punishable than the guilt of the enemy.

19,20. Once again we are warned not to get all upset over the apparent success of the ungodly, and not to envy the wicked. This time the reason given is that the prospects of the ungodly are very bad. They have nothing good to look forward to. Instead the light of their life will be extinguished.

21,22. This proverb inculcates reverence and respect for the Lord and for the king as His representative. It also warns against those who are out to change divine institutions or to overthrow civil governments. Both types of rebelliousness will bring sudden and unimaginable calamity on the guilty ones.

The Christian is taught to obey human government as long as he can do so without compromising his loyalty to the Lord. If a government orders him to disobey the Lord, then he should refuse and humbly take the consequences. Under no circumstances should he join any plot to overthrow the government.

23-26. This begins a new section of wise sayings that extends through verse 34.

It is a despicable thing to show partiality when judging matters of right and wrong. The judge who blurs moral distinctions by acquitting the guilty will be cursed by the people and hated by nations. On the other hand those judges who rebuke sin will be rewarded by God and blessed by men. Those who render honest and just verdicts will win the kiss of approval from the people.

27. Just as a man must clear away the trees and cultivate the land before building a house, so he should get his own life in order before having a family. Thus, the proverb may be a warning against rushing into marriage with all its responsibilities before a person is spiritually, emotionally, and financially prepared.

28,29. Under no circumstance should anyone bring false accusations against his neighbor or spread lies about him. Even if the neighbor has done those very things, there is no excuse for returning evil for evil.

30-34. The writer passed by the sluggard's vineyard and saw that it was overgrown with thorns. Plants with stinging hairs or nettles were everywhere to be seen. The stone wall was in ruins. There was an object lesson in this. When anyone asks for just a little more sleep, a few more winks, a few more yawns, you can be sure that poverty will overtake him like a highwayman and like an armed robber.

When we succumb to sloth in spiritual matters, our life (vineyard) becomes infested with the works of the flesh (thistles and nettles). There is no fruit for God. Our spiritual defenses (the wall) are down, and the devil gains a foothold. The result of our coldness and backsliding is poverty of soul.

CHAPTER 25

1. The proverbs contained in chapters 25-29 were composed by Solomon but put into written form years later by the men of Hezekiah, king of Judah. There are 140 proverbs corresponding to the numerical value of the letters in the Hebrew form of the name Hezekiah.

2. It is the glory of God to conceal a thing. Think of all the secrets hidden in His natural creation, in His written Word, and in His providential dealings! "He would not be God if His counsels and works did not transcend human intelligence" (Thomas Cartwright).

The honor of kings is to search out a matter. In its context, this probably means that a wise king will keep himself informed of important developments affecting his kingdom and will make full investigation in order to render true judgments and formulate sound policies.

The application for us is that we should be diligent in searching out the spiritual treasures that are concealed in the Bible.

3. The height of the heavens seems to be limitless, and the depths of the earth seem to be unsearchable. Likewise there is something inscrutable about the mind of noble kings; no one knows exactly what they are thinking.

4,5. When silver is melted in a crucible, the dross or impurities rise to the surface like scum. When this scum is removed, the silversmith has molten metal that is suitable for making a vessel. The dross here symbolizes wicked counselors in the king's court. When they are removed, the kingdom is established on a righteous basis.

The first thing Christ will do when He returns to reign will be to cleanse His kingdom of rebellion, lawlessness, and everything else that offends.

6,7. It is a wise policy not to push yourself to the forefront in the royal court, or to seek a place among celebrities. It is far better to be invited to a place of honor than to seize it and then be publicly humiliated in the king's presence.

This advice is reminiscent of Jeremiah 45:5, "Seekest thou great things for thyself? seek them not." Also the words of the Lord Jesus in Luke 14:8-10.

The last clause "whom thine eyes have seen" should possibly belong to the next verse, as in the RSV, "What your eyes have seen do not hastily bring into court. . . ."

8-10. The Bible condemns the litigious spirit, that is, the desire to rush to the lawcourt to settle every grievance. A person might tell everything he has seen and yet be put to shame when his neighbor testifies.

It is better to handle grievances privately (see Matt. 18:15), and not to blab about them to others. "A little disagreement arises with some friends, and you have not the courage to go and speak about it to that friend alone, but mention it to another. The principle laid down in God's

Word is forgotten, and mischief follows. Talking about a thing of this kind does no good, and in the end widens the breach. If we would only take such a passage as our guide, and regulate our conduct by it, we would lay aside many trivial 'causes' of offense, and spare ourselves many disturbings of mind" (author unknown).

Verse 10 contemplates the third party's rebuking you for not going directly to the offender, and your gaining a reputation as a gossip or worse.

11. An appropriate word is like apples of gold in pictures (AV) or in a setting (RSV) of silver. The right word is as morally beautiful and suitable as the combination of precious and attractive metals.

12. An earring of gold and an ornament of fine gold enhance physical beauty; so a wise reprover adds moral beauty to the one who is willing to learn.

13. Ordinarily snow would be a disaster in the time of harvest. Here it means snow added to a drink of water and given to a reaper in the harvest field.

Just as an iced drink refreshes a man on a hot day, so a faithful messenger refreshes those who sent him.

14. Whoever promises a gift but fails to deliver it is like clouds and wind which make people think rain is coming but which pass away without bringing rain.

Although this proverb does not deal with spiritual gifts, there is a valid application. A man may pretend to be a great teacher or preacher, but it is disappointing when he cannot live up to people's expectations. The Indians used to have a word for it: "Heap big wind—no rain."

15. Gentleness and patience will often persuade a prince more than if a person becomes provoked and excited. In the same way, a soft tongue can break a bone, that is, it can accomplish more than the crunch of powerful jaws and teeth.

16. Honey is good when taken in moderation, but too much of a good thing is sickening. We should eat to live, not live to eat.

"Some friends of ours have eight children, and they all love ice cream. On a hot summer day, one of the younger ones declared that she wished they could eat nothing but ice cream! The others chimed agreement, and to their surprise the father said, 'All right. Tomorrow you can have all the ice cream you want—nothing but ice cream!' The children squealed with delight, and could hardly contain themselves until the next day. They came trooping down to breakfast shouting their orders for chocolate, strawberry, or vanilla ice cream—soup bowls full! Mid-morning snack—ice cream again. Lunch—ice cream, this time slightly smaller portions. When they came in for mid-afternoon snack, their mother was just taking some fresh muffins out of the oven, and the aroma wafted through the whole house.

" 'Oh goody!' said little Teddy. 'Fresh muffins—my favorite!' He made a move for the jam cupboard, but his mother stopped him.

" 'Don't you remember? It's ice cream day—nothing but ice cream.'

" 'Oh yeah. . . .

" 'Want to sit up for a bowl?'

" 'No thanks. Just give me a one-dip cone.'

"By suppertime the enthusiasm for an all-ice-cream diet had waned considerably. As they sat staring at fresh bowls of ice cream, Mary—whose suggestion had started this whole adventure—looked up at her daddy and said, 'Couldn't we just trade in this ice cream for a crust of bread?' " (Larry Christenson).

17. Moderation applies not only to honey but to visiting. It is important to know when to leave. You can overstay your welcome.

"How much better is God's friendship than man's! We are the more welcome to God the oftener we come to Him" (Cartwright).

18. Here are three apt similes for the man who bears false witness against his neighbor:

a maul—i.e., a hammer that clubs and smashes to pieces.

a sword—with its two sharp cutting edges.

an arrow—piercing and wounding.

19. If you bite down hard with a broken tooth, you'll wish you hadn't. If you put your weight on a foot that's out of joint, it will let you down. That's exactly what it's like to put confidence in an unreliable man in time of trouble—painful and disappointing.

20. To sing songs to a heavy heart is provoking, annoying, unwelcome. It is as unsuitable as taking away a man's coat from him in cold weather, or as pouring vinegar on soda, causing violent agitation.

21,22. Paul quotes these verses in Romans 12:20. We can overcome evil with good by repaying every offense or discourtesy with a kindness.

An irate neighbor called a new believer and delivered a violent tirade against the believer's five-year-old daughter for trampled flowers, a broken window, and other offenses. When the neighbor came up for air, the Christian asked her to come over to discuss the matter.

By the time the neighbor arrived, the table had been set for coffee and sweetrolls. "Oh, I'm sorry you're having company." "No," replied the believer, "I thought we could talk about my daughter over a cup of coffee." The Christian gave thanks for the food and asked for God's wisdom. When she opened her eyes, the visitor was crying. "It's not your daughter, it's mine," blurted the neighbor. "I don't know why I lashed out at you. I just can't cope with my children, my husband, or my home!"

As soon as the neighbor made this admission, the young believer started sharing Christ. Within six weeks the neighbor and her family had been born again (Good News Broadcaster).

23. The preferred translation here is that the north wind produces rain (NASB, RSV), not drives it away. Likewise a backbiting tongue brings forth angry looks. The angry looks almost surely come from the victim of gossip and they should also come from anyone else who hears it. If people would rebuke the backbiter, he would soon go out of business.

24. This is almost identical with 21:9, repeated to emphasize the unpleasantness of living with a nagging woman.

25. The gospel is God's good news from a far country—heaven. Like cold water to a thirsty soul, the gospel is refreshing and thirst quenching.

26. When good men bow down before the wicked, when they compromise, yield, or fail to stand up for the right, it is like a muddied spring or a polluted fountain. You go looking for purity and cleanliness and are disappointed.

27. It is not good to overindulge in honey. "Beyond God's 'enough' lies nausea, not ecstasy" (Kidner).

The Hebrew of the second line is obscure. It may mean, as in the AV, "for men to search their own glory is not glory" (the "not" is supplied from the first line), or "to search into weighty matters is itself a weight" (JND), or again "to search into weighty matters is glory" (JND margin). All three make good sense.

28. A man who has never learned to discipline his life is like an undefended city, open to every kind of attack, exposed to every temptation.

CHAPTER 26

1. Snow is distinctly unseasonable in summer, and rain in harvest is injurious as well. It is equally out of place and injurious to honor fools. It is morally unfitting and only encourages them in their folly.

2. The sparrow and the swallow flit and dart in the air but never alight on us. In the same manner, an undeserved curse will never land on a person, no matter what superstition says. Balaam tried to curse Israel but couldn't (Num. 23:8; Deut. 23:5).

3. Just as it is necessary to use a whip on a horse, and a bridle on an ass, so sharp correction is the only language a fool seems to understand. "Do not be as the horse or as the mule which have no understanding, whose trappings include bit and bridle to hold them in check, otherwise they will not come near to you" (Psa. 32:9 NASB).

4,5. These two verses present an apparent contradiction. The first says not to answer a fool, the second says to answer him. What is the explanation? The latter part of each verse holds the key.

Don't answer a fool in such a manner that you become a fool in the process. Don't lose your temper, or behave rudely, or speak unadvisedly.

But answer a fool. Don't let him off with his folly altogether. Reprove and rebuke him, as his folly deserves, so he will not be wise in his own conceit.

6. To send a message by the hand of a fool is to work against your own best interests. It's like cutting off your own legs or drinking poison. The fool won't deliver the message properly. He will only cause you grief. To cut off the feet means to render oneself helpless.

7. The legs of a paralyzed man hang limp and useless (see NASB). That's the way it is with a wise saying in the mouth of a fool. It is useless to him because he doesn't know when, where, or how to apply it.

8. You shouldn't bind a stone in a sling; it should be free for release. It is just as absurd to give honor to a fool.

A second possible meaning is that just as a stone is soon parted from a slingshot, so a fool will quickly prove himself unworthy of any honor that is bestowed upon him.

9. When a drunkard handles thorns, they are painful and dangerous to himself and others. So a parable in the mouth of a fool can be misapplied and distorted. He might use it to justify his folly and to draw false conclusions concerning others.

10. The Hebrew text of this verse is very obscure, as is seen by the variety of translations:

"Like an archer who wounds everyone, so is he who hires a fool or who hires those who pass by" (NASB).

"Like an archer who wounds everybody is he who hires a passing fool or drunkard" (RSV).

"A master roughly worketh everyone: he both hireth the fool and hireth passers-by" (JND).

"A master performs all things, but he who hires a fool hires a passer-by" (Berkeley).

"The law settles quarrels at last, yet silence the fool, and feud there shall be none" (Knox).

"An employee who hires any fool that comes along is only hurting everyone concerned" (TEV).

It is impossible to say which meaning is correct.

11. A dog is no more revolted by its own vomit than a fool by his folly; they both go back to that which is repulsive and disgusting. This verse is applied in 2 Peter 2:22 to people who experience moral reformation but who are never truly born again. Eventually they revert to their old ways.

12. A conceited person is above correction or instruction or rebuke. It is hopeless to try to correct him. An ignorant fool can sometimes be helped by a beating, but the conceited man is impervious to advice.

13-16. Here is the sluggard again and the imaginary lion that prevents his going to work. He turns, like a hinge, on his bed. Now he lies on his back, now on his front. Back and forth he swings with plenty of motion but no progress toward getting up. Later when he is at the table, he dips his hand in the dish (NASB) but can't muster up enough energy to lift the food to his mouth. Even something as pleasurable as eating is an exhausting effort. He is wiser in his own eyes than seven men who can give a proper answer, that is, seven intelligent men, unanimous in their insistence that he is wrong, wouldn't change his mind a fraction.

17. The passer-by who vexes himself (ASV) or meddles (NASB) with quarrels that are none of his business is asking for trouble. It's like grabbing a dog by the ears; you don't dare hold on and you don't dare let go.

18,19. Like a lunatic who shoots firebrands and deadly arrows is the man who deals treacherously with his neighbor and then, when the harm is done, says, "I was just kidding." It is like excusing murder as a joke. This proverb could be applied to irresponsible courtship and engagement.

20,21. Just as fuel feeds a fire, so gossip feeds trouble. A woman in Brooklyn said to her neighbor, "Tilly told me that you told her that secret I told you not to tell her." The other replied, "She's a mean thing. I told Tilly not to tell you I told her." The first speaker responded, "Well, I told Tilly I wouldn't tell you she told me, so don't tell her I did."

Unless a troublemaker keeps adding aggravations and gossip and lies, strife will soon die out.

22. This is a repetition of 18:8. "Wounds" should be "dainty morsels." Fallen human nature eats up gossip as if it were tasty tidbits.

23-26. "Like the glaze covering an earthen vessel are smooth lips with an evil heart" (RSV). A shining, silvery finish disguises the worthlessness and drabness of the earthenware pottery underneath. So lips burning with pretended love often cover a heart full of hatred. The pretended affection of Judas, the betrayer, illustrates the point.

The chronic hater tries to hide his enmity with gracious words, at the same time storing up deceit within. Though he may speak graciously, you can't trust him. He hides seven abominations in his heart, that is, he is full of evil and malice. Though his hatred may be hidden for the time by deceit, eventually his wickedness will be manifested before all.

27. Man's evil recoils upon himself, just as Louis the Strong's workmanship did. He was asked to make chains that would hold the most desperate prisoners during one of the early French wars. He tempered some very fine steel and made chains that were unparalleled for strength.

Later Louis himself was found guilty of treason and sent to prison. He was heard to moan, "These are my own chains! If I had known I was forging them for myself, how differently I would have made them!"

28. This proverb castigates the slanderer and the flatterer. The first one hates his victims, the second works ruin on his.

Lesson Eleven
Proverbs 27—29

CHAPTER 27

1. No one is sure of tomorrow. Therefore, don't brag about all you will do, like the rich fool did (Luke 12:16-21). See also James 4:13-15.

2. It is poor taste and very inelegant to praise yourself. A truly refined person tries to keep himself in the background, while praising others. "Beware of autobiographies" (Berkeley margin).

3. The persistent, provocative remarks of a fool are harder to put up with than a heavy physical burden. A man would rather carry stone or sand than be constantly annoyed by a loud-mouthed fool.

4. Wrath and anger are cruel and overwhelming, yet often they are short-lived. But jealousy continually gnaws away at a person and is therefore more grievous. This would apply, for instance, to one whose marriage has been disrupted by a third person.

5. An outright rebuke benefits the recipient but no one benefits from secret love, that is, love that refuses to point out a person's failings.

6. Most people do not want to be honest with you about your faults; they are afraid that you will turn against them. It is a true friend who is willing to risk your goodwill in order to help you by constructive criticism.

The kisses of an enemy are deceitful (AV), or better, profuse (RSV).

Judas gave a sign to the mob in advance to help them distinguish Jesus from the disciples; the sign was a kiss. The universal symbol of love was to be prostituted to its lowest use.

As he approached the Lord, Judas said, "Hail, Master!" then kissed Him profusely. Two different words for *kiss* are used (Matt. 26:48,49). The first, in verse 48, is the normal word for kiss. But in verse 49, a stronger word is used, expressing repeated, passionate kissing.

7. A man who is overfed loses his appreciation of the choicest, sweetest foods. A hungry person is grateful for the slimmest pickings.

This is true of material possessions and of spiritual privileges.

8. The man who wanders from his home is the one who is discontented and restless. He has the wanderlust. He is like a bird that strays from its nest, shirking responsibilities and failing to build anything solid and substantial.

9. The pleasantness of perfumes and ointment is compared to the fragrance of loving advice from a friend. There is something truly heartwarming about fellowship with a friend.

10. Friendships must be cultivated and kept alive. Often the oldest friends are the best. So don't lose touch with your friends or old friends of the family.

"Neither go into thy brother's house." The brother here is obviously one who has been offended, one who is far off. When trouble comes, you will get more help and sympathy from a faithful neighbor than from a near relative who is estranged from you.

11. A son's behavior reflects on his father's instruction. A disciple brings either joy or shame to his teacher. Berkeley's footnote says it well: "The teacher's one defense—the success of his students."

12. Noah was a prudent man, hiding himself and his family in the ark. The rest of the people went on their way carelessly and indifferently and suffered for it. (See notes on 22:3.)

13. In modern idiom the first line means that the man who is surety for a stranger will "lose his shirt."

The second line should probably read, "and hold him in pledge when he gives surety for foreigners." In other words, be sure you have a legal claim on the property of anyone who will guarantee the debts of strangers, for if the debtor can't pay, the surety will have to.

14. A man doesn't appreciate loud, flattering greetings early in the morning when he is trying to sleep. They are more of a nuisance than a blessing.

15.,16. The continual drip, drip, drip of water through the roof on a very rainy day has this in common with a scolding, nagging wife. They are both enough to "drive a person up the wall."

"To restrain her is to restrain the wind or to grasp oil in one's right hand" (RSV). No matter what you say, she will evade, excuse, blame others—and go right on nagging.

17. It used to be common to see the host at a table sharpening the carving knife by drawing each side of the cutting edge against a hardened steel rod with fine ridges. Just as the action of iron against iron sharpens, so the interchange of ideas among men makes these men more acute in their thinking. Sharing each other's opinions gives a helpful breadth of view. Asking questions sharpens wits. Friendly intercommunication hones the personality.

18. The one who takes good care of a fig tree is rewarded by a good crop. Diligence in attending to one's occupation insures food in the pantry or deepfreeze.

It is also true that the one who faithfully serves his employer will be honored. Jesus said, "If any man serve me, him will my Father honor" (John 12:26).

19. As you look into a clear pool, you see your face reflected in the water. Even so, as you study other people, you see much that you find in yourself—the same emotions, temptations, ambitions, thoughts, strengths, and weaknesses.

That is why it happens that if a man preaches to himself, he is surprised by how many other people he hits.

20. Sheol and Abaddon, death and the grave never reach the point where they don't claim more victims. So the eyes of men are never satisfied by anything the world has to offer.

Tolstoy tells of a farmer who had a lust for more and more land. "Finally he heard of cheap land among the Bashkirs. He sold all he had, made a long journey to their territory, and arranged a deal with them. For one thousand rubles he could buy all the land he could walk around in one day. The next morning he set out and walked far in one direction and then turned left. He made many detours to include extra areas of good soil. By the time he made his last turn, he realized he had gone too far. He ran as fast as possible to get back to the starting point before sunset. Faster and faster he ran and finally staggered and fell across the starting point just as the sun set. He lay there dead. They buried him in a small hole, all the land he needed" (Arthur G. Gish).

It should be added that the craving of man's heart is fully satisfied in Christ.

Show me Thy face—one transient gleam
    of loveliness Divine
And I shall never think or dream
    of other love save Thine;
All lesser light will darken quite,
    all lower glories wane,
The beautiful of earth will scarce
    seem beautiful again.

21. As a fining pot or crucible tests silver, and a furnace tests gold, so "a man is tried by his praise" (ASV). This may mean that a man is tested by how he reacts to praise. Does it go to his head and ruin him, or does he accept it calmly and humbly?

Or it may mean that a man is tested by the things that he praises (ASV margin). His standards or sense of values are a reflection of his character.

Or again it might mean, "So let a man be to his praise," that is, "let him purify it from all the alloy of flattery and baseness with which it is too probably mixed up" (Barnes).

22. You have probably seen a mortar and pestle on display in a drug store. The mortar is a bowl-shaped object. The pestle is a short, thick rod with a globular end and is used for pounding or pulverizing things in the mortar.

Even if you could put a fool in a mortar with wheat and pound both with the pestle, you wouldn't be able to separate the fool and his foolishness. In other words, you can separate the wheat from the chaff, but folly in a fool is ineradicable.

23-27. This paragraph extols the virtues of agricultural life, but puts ample stress on the importance of the farmer's diligence.

Unwearied and unceasing care must be exercised in tending the flocks and herds. Pastoral prosperity can only be maintained by constant diligence. This applies with equal force to the shepherding of sheep in a local church.

Riches do not last and the honors of royalty soon pass away unless constant care is exercised in attending to one's affairs.

There is tremendous satisfaction for the farmer in seeing the crops appearing, and in harvesting the vegetation from the hills. The lambs provide wool for clothing, and by selling goats he can buy additional fields. There is plenty of food for his family and for his servants.

CHAPTER 28

1. A guilty conscience makes a man jump at the slightest noise. People with a clear conscience don't have to drive with one eye on the rearview mirror; they are as bold as a lion.

2. When a land is guilty of widespread transgression, it suffers frequent changes of government. When the ruler is a man of integrity and understanding, the country enjoys a settled, stable condition.

The Northern kingdom (Israel) had 19 kings in the space of about 200 years.

3. A poor man who rises to a position of wealth and power is often more oppressive on the poor than people from a higher income level would be. He is like a sweeping rain that levels fields of grain, that destroys the crops instead of helping them to grow.

4. People who throw off the restraint of God's law and of civil law often praise the ungodly. This, of course, is an attempt to justify themselves.

Those who keep the law oppose the transgressors and speak out for the cause of righteousness.

5. Wicked men do not understand justice; by refusing to practice it, they lose the power to understand it.

Those who seek the Lord's will are given proper powers of discernment. There is a close link between morality and understanding (see Psalm 119:100).

6. A poor man who lives a clean, honest life is better than a rich man who is crooked in his ways, who pretends to be living a good life while all the time practicing deceit and treachery.

7. A law-abiding son is wise. One who associates with gluttons and drunkards (see NASB) brings disgrace on his father.

8. Under the law of Moses, a Jew was forbidden to charge usury (interest) to another Jew. He could charge it to a Gentile but not to a fellow-Jew (Deut. 23:19,20). Today usury means *exorbitant* rates of interest.

Those who enrich themselves by usury or other forms of illicit revenue will lose their wealth; it will be taken from them and given to someone who knows how to use it better and how to treat the poor considerately.

9. If a man will not hear and obey the law of God, God will not hear his prayer. Actually his prayer is hateful to God.

> I may as well kneel down
> And worship gods of stone
> As offer to the Living God
> A prayer of words alone.

10. Whoever tempts the righteous to fall into sin will fall into a pit of punishment. Jesus warned, "whoso shall offend one of these little ones which believe in me, it were better for him that a millstone were hanged about his neck, and that he were drowned in the depth of the sea" (Matt. 18:6).

"But the blameless will inherit good" (NASB). The blameless here may mean those who lead others in paths of holiness rather than sin. Or it may mean those who refuse to be victimized by solicitations to sin.

11. A rich man who glories in his riches thinks he is very clever. Priding himself on his rare financial acumen, he is wise in his own conceit. He confuses riches and wisdom.

A poor man with understanding can see through such pretension. Charles Lamb once approached one of those swaggering men with the remark, "Excuse me, sire, but are you—anybody in particular?"

12. When righteous rulers rise to power, there is great rejoicing. When wicked rulers triumph, men hide themselves for fear (see NASB, ASV, RSV).

13. There are two kinds of forgiveness, judicial and parental. When we trust Christ as Lord and Savior, we receive forgiveness from the penalty of sins; that is judicial forgiveness. When we, as believers, confess our sins, we receive parental forgiveness (1 John 1:9); this maintains fellowship with God our Father.

There is no blessing for the man who covers his sins, that is, who refuses to drag them out into the light and to confess them to God and to anyone else who has been wronged. But anyone who confesses and forsakes his sins has the assurance that God not only forgives but forgets (Heb. 10:17).

14. One element of true happiness is to have a tender heart before the Lord. It is the one who becomes hard and unrepentant who falls into trouble. God can resist the proud and brazen but He cannot resist a broken and contrite heart.

15. Beastlike and inhumane describes the tyrant who rides herd over poor, weak, and defenseless people. He is like a roaring lion and a rampaging bear.

16. Apparently the prince described here is one who lacks understanding in the sense that he seeks to enrich himself at all costs. This man is also a great oppressor because he tramples on others to get richer. The ruler who hates covetousness, who lives unselfishly for the good of his people will prolong his days.

17. "A man that is laden with the blood of any person shall flee unto the pit; let no man stay him" (ASV). The wilful murderer is a fugitive, racing toward his doom. No one should seek to obstruct or interfere with justice. God has said, "Whoso sheddeth man's blood, by man shall his blood be shed" (Gen. 9:6).

18. The first line refers to salvation from damage in this life, not from damnation in the next. Eternal salvation from the penalty of sin is not obtained by walking uprightly but by faith in the Lord Jesus Christ. The upright walk is a fruit of that salvation. But the man who does live righteously is saved from many a snare in this life.

The man who vacillates from one form of crookedness to another will go down in one fell swoop.

19. The contrast here is between plenty of food and plenty of poverty (see RSV). The diligent farmer has the former. The one who engages in empty, non-productive activities has the latter.

20. A faithful man here is one who is honest and who does not covet great wealth. He will be richly blessed. The man who seeks to enrich himself quickly by unscrupulous means will be punished.

21. It is rank injustice for a judge to show partiality, and yet a man will often do this for a crust of bread, that is, for the most trifling consideration.

22. A miserly, grudging, ungenerous man races after wealth, little realizing that poverty will soon overtake him.

23. When a friend lovingly rebukes you, it is hard to take at the time. It hurts your pride. But afterwards you realize that this friend must really have cared for you to point out your faults, and so you are grateful to him.

Flattery may seem pleasant at the time, but eventually you realize that it wasn't true anyway, and that the person was simply trying to gain your favor. He probably flatters everyone he meets.

24. A son who robs his parents might excuse it on the grounds that it will be his eventually, or that he has dedicated it to the Lord in the meantime (Mark 7:11). But God is not deceived; He puts that person in the same class as a robber or murderer.

25. The grasping or greedy man (ASV) stirs up strife, perhaps by pushing everyone else aside in his futile race for riches or power or preeminence (see Jas. 4:1). It is the God-fearing man who succeeds in finding peace and satisfaction.

26. He who trusts his own wisdom to guide him through life is a fool. He is casting his anchor inside the boat, and thus will drift incessantly. The one who looks to the Lord for guidance acts wisely (see Jer. 9:23,24).

27. God will reward those who show mercy to the poor. The man who turns away his eyes from genuine cases of need will have many a sorrow.

28. When wicked men rise to power, the populace hides itself for fear. But when wicked rulers are overthrown, the righteous come out of hiding.

CHAPTER 29

1. A man who continues in sin, in spite of repeated warnings, will suddenly be destroyed, without hope of any further opportunity. The people who lived before the flood refused to listen to Noah. The flood came and they were destroyed.

An acquaintance of mine who had repeatedly rejected the gospel invitation met a Christian lady who had prayed for him often. She said, "Don't you think it's time you turned to the Lord?" He answered, "What has He ever done for me?" That weekend his life was snuffed out in a mysterious mishap. It was one of those accidents that couldn't happen—but did!

2. The character of a nation's rulers affects the morale of the country. When the righteous increase (NASB), that is, in numbers and in power, the populace rejoices. Wicked rulers cause widespread mourning.

3. A son who loves wisdom, who lives a dedicated, separated Christian life, brings joy to his father. But the son who lives in immorality squanders his father's money. The prodigal son, you remember, wasted his father's substance in riotous living.

4. By acting with justice, a king brings his country to a position of strength. The one who accepts bribes to pervert justice is undermining the stability of the government.

5. The flatterer imperils his neighbor by refusing to tell him the truth or by praising him for things that are not true. Also he encourages pride which leads to a fall.

6. An ungodly man is often caught in the net of his own sin. The righteous man is happy because he does not have to fear the consequences of transgression. He moves forward with singing and rejoicing.

7. Upright people take an active interest in the welfare of the poor. The ungodly are not interested in showing any such concern.

8. Scorners set a city aflame (see NASB). They create turmoil by arousing tempers, agitating the people, and creating divisions. Wise men seek to avert discord and promote peace.

9. This proverb may have two meanings. The more probable is this: When a wise man argues with a fool, the fool will only rage and laugh (see NASB, RSV, Berkeley). He will never be persuaded, and there will be no peace.

The other interpretation is that when a wise man argues with a fool, whether the wise man uses severity or humor, it doesn't make any difference. Nothing positive is accomplished.

10. Again there are two possible interpretations. One is set forth in the ASV: "The bloodthirsty hate him that is perfect; and, as for the upright, they seek his life." Here the bloodthirsty are the wicked aggressors in each case.

The other meaning is found in the NASB, JND, and Berkeley. Here the bloodthirsty are found destroying life in the first line, but the upright are seen seeking to preserve and protect it, in the second line.

11. "A fool gives full vent to his anger, but the wise man, holding it back, quiets it" (Berkeley). "The idea of allowing anger to break out in an undisciplined manner by saying or doing whatever comes into mind without weighing the consequences, without counting ten, without holding it back and quieting it, without hearing the whole story, is totally wrong" (Jay Adams).

12. The thought here seems to be that if a ruler wants to be pampered and flattered and comforted by pleasant news, then all his servants will treat him exactly that way. They will lie and flatter.

13. There may be a great gulf between the poor and the oppressor in human society, but they meet on a common level before God. It is He who gives light to their eyes.

14. In judging a ruler, God is especially interested in whether he treats the poor considerately and without prejudice. If so, He promises to establish his throne forever. Actually we know only one such ruler; His name is Jesus.

15. This proverb flatly contradicts many modern specialists who advocate "permissive democracy." The rod is corporal punishment; reproof is verbal correction. These two forms of parental discipline impart wisdom. They do not inhibit a child or warp his personality as the experts say.

16. When wicked men grow more numerous and powerful, the crime rate rises. But the righteous will live to see their downfall. Of course there are exceptions, but they are the exceptions that prove the rule.

17. A child who has been disciplined properly will bring joy and rest to his parents instead of anxiety and heartache.

18. "Where there is no vision, the people cast off restraint; but he that keepeth the law, happy is he" (ASV). "Vision" here means prophetic revelation, hence the Word of God (see 1 Sam. 3:1). The thought is that when God's Word is not known and honored, the people run wild.

The ones who obey the law, that is, the Word of God, are the truly blessed ones.

19. This verse seems to describe the obstinate, intractable attitude of many slaves. Oral orders are not always enough. They may understand the master's instructions but they don't always carry them out. They just remain silent and sullen.

Jesus said, "Why call ye me, Lord, Lord, and do not the

things which I say?" (Luke 6:46).

20. Of all the subjects dealt with in Proverbs, our speech comes in for a lion's share of attention. Here we learn that the man who speaks before he thinks is more hopeless than a fool. This puts him in the same class as the man who is wise in his own conceits (26:12).

21. If you pamper and spoil a slave he will forget his proper position and will soon expect you to treat him like a son. Undue familiarity in the employer-employee relationship often breeds contempt.

The word translated "son" in the second line is of very uncertain meaning.

22. Most of us have met these two men at one time or another. The angry man stirs up all kinds of trouble, and the passionate man commits plenty of sins.

23. A proud man can be sure of being brought low. It is the humble man who is elevated to a place of honor.

Professor Smith was climbing the Weisshorn. When near the top the guide stood aside to permit the traveler to have the honor of first reaching the top. Exhilarated by the view, forgetful of the fierce gale that was blowing, he sprang up and stood erect on the summit. The guide pulled him down, exclaiming, "On your knees sir; you are not safe there except on your knees." Life's summits, whether of knowledge, of love, or of worldly success, are full of perils (Choice Gleanings).

> O Lamb of God, still keep me
> Close to Thy pierced side;
> 'Tis only there in safety
> And peace I can abide.

24. An accomplice of a thief acts as if he hates his own soul. Why? Because when "he heareth cursing," that is, when the judge puts him under oath to tell all he knows, "he betrayeth it not," that is, he does not testify. Under the law of Moses, a man who heard the judge putting him under oath and yet refused to testify, was counted guilty and was punished accordingly (see Lev. 5:1). There was no such thing as "pleading the Fifth Amendment."

25. The fear of man results in yielding to human pressure to commit evil or to refrain from doing what is right. How many have gone to hell because they were afraid of what their friends would say if they trusted Christ!

The man who trusts in the Lord is safe, come what may.

Thought: "We fear man so much because we fear God so little" (Gurnall).

26. Many people look to an earthly ruler as if he were the solution to all their problems. But it is from the Lord that justice comes.

27. There is no rapport between the wicked and the upright. The just look with disfavor on the ungodly, and the wicked abominate the upright. Just as a straight stick shows up a crooked one, so the contrast between a clean life and a wicked one is glaring.

The proverbs of Solomon end at this point.

Lesson Twelve
Proverbs 30,31

CHAPTER 30

1. All we know about Agur is found in this chapter. He introduces himself as the son of Jakeh.

The words "even the prophecy" (oracle, ASV) may also be translated "of Massa" (RSV). This would identify Agur as a descendant of Ishmael (Gen. 25:14).

The second line may also read, "The man said, 'I have wearied myself, O God, I have wearied myself, O God, and am consumed'" (ASV margin). This leads naturally into what follows—the impossibility of the infinitesimal comprehending the Infinite.

2. Agur begins with a confession of his own inability to attain to understanding. Apparently it is a statement of genuine humility—a proper attitude for anyone who would inquire into the works and ways of God.

3. He does not profess to have learned wisdom or to have found God by human searching. He recognizes that he does not have the power in himself to attain to the knowledge of the Holy One.

4. By a series of questions, he sets forth the greatness of God as He is revealed in nature.

The first describes God as having access to the heights and depth of the universe where no man can follow Him. The second points out His control over the massive power of the winds. Third is His might in containing the waters, either in clouds above the earth or in the ocean beds. Next is His establishment of the boundaries of the land masses.

What is His name, and what is His Son's name? The thought is, "Who can ever fully know such a great Being, so incomprehensible, so mysterious, so powerful, so omnipresent?" The answer is "No one can ever understand Him fully."

But we do know that His name is God, and His Son's name is the Lord Jesus Christ.

5. Agur now turns from the revelation of God in nature to His revelation in the Word. He asserts the infallibility of the sacred Scriptures—"every word of God is pure." Then he speaks of the security of all who trust in the God of the Bible—"He is a shield unto them that put their trust in Him."

6. The absolute sufficiency of the Scriptures is asserted next. No man should dare to add his thoughts and speculations to what God has spoken.

This verse condemns the cults who give their own writings and traditions the same authority as the Bible.

7. Verses 7-9 contain the only prayer in the book of Proverbs. The prayer is short and to the point. It contains two petitions, one covering the spiritual life (v. 8a) and the other covering the physical life (vv. 8b,9).

8. First Agur wanted his life to be worthwhile and honest. He didn't want it to be wasted on trivia. He didn't want to major on minors. And he didn't want to deceive others or to be deceived.

As to the physical, he asked to be delivered from the extremes of poverty and riches. He would be satisfied with the provision of His daily needs. He was saying, in effect, "Give me this day my daily bread."

9. He gives reasons for wanting to avoid the twin extremes of affluence and poverty. If he were full, he might become independent of the Lord and deny Him by not feeling any great need for Him. He might be emboldened to say, "Who is the Lord?"—that is, who is He that I should look to Him for what I need or want?

The peril of poverty would be that he might steal, and then, to cover up, he might deny under oath that he had done it.

10. In what seems to be an abrupt transition, Agur warns against slandering a servant to his master. The penalty would be that the curse he pronounces against you would come to pass because God is the Defender of the oppressed.

The New Testament warns us against judging servants of the Lord; to their own Master they stand or fall (Rom. 14:4).

11-14. The generation described here bears striking resemblance to the generation living today and to the one which will exist in the last days (2 Tim. 3:1-7). Notice the following features:

1. Disrespectful to parents (v. 11). They curse their father and show no gratitude to their mother, thus breaking the Fifth Commandment. The hostility of young people toward their parents is one of the chief characteristics of our decadent society.

2. Self-righteous (v. 12). These people are vile and unclean, yet they have no sense of shame. Outwardly they appear like whitewashed sepulchers but inwardly they are full of dead men's bones.

3. Pride and arrogance (v. 13). They resemble Rabbi Simeon Ben Jochai who said, "If there are only two righteous men in the world, I and my son are the two. If only one, I am he."

4. Fiercely oppressive (v. 14). In their insatiable greed for wealth, they rip, tear, and devour the poor by long hours, low wages, miserable working conditions, and other forms of social injustice.

15,16. The greed of the oppressors in the preceding verse leads on to other examples of desires that are never satisfied.

1. The horseleach (AV), or vampire (ASV margin), (v. 15) is pictured as having two daughters who have an endless capacity for sucking blood.

2. The grave (v. 16a) never says "No vacancy." Death never takes a holiday, and the grave never fails to accommodate its victims.

3. The barren womb (v. 16b) is never willing to accept its sterility but hopes continually for motherhood.

4. The earth that is not filled with water (v. 16c), no matter how much rain falls. It can always absorb some more.

5. A fire (v. 16d) never says "Enough." It will devour as much fuel as a person wants to feed it.

The expression "There are three things . . . yea, four . . ." is a literary formula used to produce a sense of climax. Four is the number of weakness, of the creature in contrast to the Creator.

17. This proverb seems to be isolated from the rest, though similar to verse 11. It teaches that a son who mocks his father and disobeys his mother will die a violent death and will be denied a decent burial. To the Jewish mind, it was a great tragedy and disgrace for a body to be unburied. The fate of the wayward son is for his carcass to be devoured by vultures.

18-20. Agur lists four things that were too wonderful for him. As we study them, we have a vague suspicion that there is a spiritual analogy beneath the surface, but what is that analogy and what is the common thread that ties them together? Most commentators suggest that these four things leave no trace behind them. This seems to be confirmed by the way the adulterous woman in verse 20 is able to hide her guilt. Kidner says that the common denominator is "the easy mastery, by the appropriate agent, of elements as difficult to negotiate as air, rock, sea—and young woman."

1. "The way of an eagle in the air" (v. 19a). Here we face the marvel of flight. The gracefulness and speed of the eagle are proverbial.

2. "The way of a serpent upon a rock" (v. 19b). The wonder here is the movement of a reptile without benefit of legs, arms, or wings.

3. "The way of a ship in the midst of the sea" (v. 19c). It is possible that the ship here may be a poetic name for fish (see also Psa. 104:26), and that Agur is marvelling at the

navigational finesse of marine life.

4. "The way of a man with a maid" (v. 19d). The simplest explanation of this expression refers it to the instinct of courtship. Some, however, take a less idyllic view and apply it to the seduction of a virgin.

A fifth wonder, apparently thrown in for good measure, is the way an adulterous woman can satisfy her lust, then wipe her mouth and protest her complete innocence (v. 20).

21-23. Four insufferable things are next listed; they are the kind of things that throw the earth into turmoil.

1. A slave when he reigns (v. 22a). He becomes arrogant and overbearing, drunk with his new position.

2. A well-fed fool (v. 22b). His prosperity causes him to be more insolent than ever.

3. A hated woman who finally succeeds in getting married (v. 23a). Her wretched disposition would normally have kept her single, but by some fluke, she lands a husband. Then she becomes imperious and haughty, taunting those who are still unmarried.

4. A servant-girl who inherits her mistress's fortune (v. 23b). She doesn't know how to act with refinement and grace, but is coarse, rude, and vulgar.

24-28. Now Agur turns to four things that are wise out of all proportion to their size.

1. The ants (v. 25) are tiny creatures and seemingly helpless, yet they busy themselves during the summer months, but not to provide for the winter, because, according to the World Book, "Ants cluster together and spend the winter sleeping inside their nests."

2. The conies (v. 26 AV), or badgers (NASB), or marmots (Moffatt), feeble as they are, yet they have the wisdom to find protection in the rocks. Cleft rocks provide the best protection. The spiritual application is found in the hymn, "Rock of Ages, cleft for me."

3. The locusts (v. 27) have no visible ruler, yet the order in which they move is remarkable.

4. The spider (v. 28 AV), or lizard (NASB), is small

enough to be held in the hand (see NASB), yet it succeeds in getting into king's palaces. Its access to unlikely and important places is often duplicated by Christians today. God does not leave Himself without a witness, even in courts of royalty.

29-31. The final series has to do with four examples of stately, graceful movement.

1. The lion (v. 30), the king of beasts, is majestic and unruffled as it walks.

2. There is considerable uncertainty about the second example (v. 31a). It may be a greyhound (AV), a strutting cock (NASB), or a warhorse (JND margin). All these fit the description of lofty dignity.

3. A ram or he-goat (v. 31b) is a picture of noble bearing as it strides at the head of a flock.

4. There is also some doubt about the fourth example (v. 31c), whether it should read "a king, against whom there is no rising up" (AV), or "a king when his army is with him" (NASB), or "a king striding before his people" (RSV). In any case, the point is clear that the king marches with regal dignity.

32,33. The chapter closes with two verses that seem strangely unrelated to what has preceded. Williams paraphrases the verses: "if feeble man in his folly has lifted up himself against God, or even indulged hard thoughts of Him, let him listen to the voice of wisdom and lay his hand upon his mouth; for otherwise there will be a result as surely as there is a result when milk is churned, the nose wrung, or anger excited."

CHAPTER 31

1. We have no way of knowing who King Lemuel was. His name means "dedicated to God" or "belonging to God."

The important thing is that he has preserved for us the wise counsel which his mother gave him (vv. 1-9).

2. We might fill in the thought here as follows: "What shall I say to you, and what gems of wisdom will I pass on to you, my son, whom I have dedicated to the Lord?"

3. First is a warning to avoid a life of dissipation and sensual lust. "The temptations of the harem were then, as now, the curse of all Eastern kingdoms" (Speaker's Commentary).

4-9. Second is a plea to refrain from the excessive use of wine and strong drink (v. 4). The danger for kings is that their ability to judge and to make proper decisions might be impaired by drinking. They might forget the standards of justice demanded by the law and fail to uphold the rights of the downtrodden (v. 5). The medicinal use of wine is sanctioned as a stimulant for the dying and an anti-depressant for the despondent (v. 6). It is all right for people like these to drink, and to forget their need and their misery (v. 7). But the king should be a responsible spokesman for all who cannot defend themselves, and plead the cause of all who are left desolate (v. 8). He should speak up on behalf of the poor and the needy (v. 9).

10-31. The closing section of the book describes the ideal wife. It is written in the form of an acrostic, each verse beginning with a letter of the Hebrew alphabet in proper order. Knox's translation reproduces this acrostic style in English.

A virtuous or fine wife is one who is capable, diligent, worthy, and good. Her value cannot be measured in terms of costly jewels (v. 10). Her husband can have full confidence in her, with no need to fear any lack of honest gain (v. 11). Her finest efforts are put forth to help him; she never fails to cooperate (v. 12). She is always on the lookout for wool and flax, and enjoys converting them into cloth (v. 13). On her shopping trips, she is like the merchant ships that return to port laden with produce. See her going to the supermarket, loading her shopping cart with the best bargains (v. 14).

She gets up before daybreak to prepare food for the household. The portion she gives to the maidens may include not only their breakfast but their work assignments for the day (v. 15). When she hears that some nearby land is for sale, she goes out to see it. It is just what she needs, so she buys it, then industriously plants a vineyard with money she has earned (v. 16). She prepares herself for her tasks with great vigor and enthusiasm. She is not afraid of strenuous work (v. 17). She takes a quiet, humble satisfaction in the results of her labor. After the others have gone to bed, she often works late into the night (v. 18). She reaches forth to the distaff and her hands hold the spindle, that is, she busies herself spinning wool and flax into yarn and thread (v. 19).

In addition to all this, she finds time to help those who are in need. She unselfishly shares with those who are less fortunate (v. 20). She does not dread the approach of winter because there is plenty of warm clothing in the closets (v. 21). She makes coverings (or cushions, ASV margin) for herself; her own clothing is fine linen and purple (v. 22 NASB). Her husband is a man of prominence in the community. He sits at the gate with the elders. He can devote himself to public affairs without worrying about conditions at home (v. 23).

His wife weaves fine linen, then sells it at the market. She also earns money by selling girdles or sashes to the merchants (v. 24). Clothed with industry and dignity, she faces the future with confidence (v. 25). The instruction she gives to her family is a balance of wisdom and kindness (v. 26). She keeps close touch with the affairs of her household, and does not waste time or engage in shallow, unproductive activity (v. 27).

Her children realize that she is an outstanding mother, and they tell her so. Her husband also praises her as a God-given wife (v. 28). He says, "There are many good wives in the world, but you're the best one of all" (v. 29).

The writer now adds his amen to what the husband has

just said. It is true. A woman may have charm but no common sense. She may be beautiful but impractical. But a God-fearing woman, as described above, is the best kind (v. 30). Let her be honored for her diligence and noble character. When the town fathers meet at the civic center, let them rehearse her outstanding accomplishments (v. 31).

BIBLIOGRAPHY

Adams, Jay. *Competent to Counsel*. Grand Rapids: Baker Book House, 1970.

Adolph, Paul Ernest. "God in Medical Practice," a chapter in *The Evidence of God in an Expanding Universe* by John Clover Monsma. Bangalore, India: Thomas Samuel, 1968.

Barnes, Albert. *Notes on the Old Testament, Proverbs—Ezekiel*. Grand Rapids: Baker Book House, 1972.

Bosch, Henry, Editor. *Our Daily Bread*. Grand Rapids: Radio Bible Fellowship.

Brock, Paul. "Your Emotions Can Make You Ill." Reader's Digest, Sept. 1974.

Christenson, Larry. *The Christian Family*. Minn.: Bethany Fellowship, 1970.

Davidson, F., Stibbs, A. M., Kevan, E. F. *The New Bible Commentary*. Chicago: InterVarsity Christian Fellowship, 1953.

Gish, Arthur. *Beyond the Rat Race*. Scottsdale, Pa.: Herald Press, 1973.

Griffiths, Michael. *Take My Life*. Downers Grove, Il.: InterVarsity Press, 1967.

Henry, Matthew. *Commentary on the Whole Bible*. Grand Rapids: Zondervan Publishing House, 1961.

The Pulpit Commentary, Vol. 9. Grand Rapids: Wm. B. Eerdmans Publishing Company.

Commentary on the Holy Bible (Speaker's Commentary). London: John Murray, 1873.

Daily Notes of the Scripture Union.

Choice Gleanings Calendar. Grand Rapids: Gospel Folio Press.

Jamieson, Robert; Fausset, A. R.; Brown, David. *A Commentary Critical, Experimental and Practical on the Old and New Testaments, Vol. III, Job-Isaiah*. Grand Rapids: Wm. B. Eerdmans Publishing Company, 1961.

Kidner, Derek. *The Proverbs*. London: The Tyndale Press, 1972.

Lewis, C. S. *Mere Christianity*. New York: Macmillan Company, 1960.

Morgan, J. Campbell. *Searchlights from the Word*. London: Oliphants, 1970.

Nee, Watchman. *Do All To The Glory of God*. New York: Christian Fellowship Publishers, Inc., 1974.

Williams, George. *The Student's Commentary on the Holy Scriptures*. Grand Rapids: Kregel Publications, 1953.